MINDFULNESS FOR TEENS
IN 10 MINUTES A DAY

Exercises to Feel Calm,
Stay Focused & Be Your Best Self

MINDFULNESS
for TEENS

IN 10 MINUTES A DAY

Jennie Marie Battistin
MA, LMFT

Illustrations by Clare Owen

ROCKRIDGE
PRESS

Interior and Cover Designer: Rachel Haeseker
Art Producer: Sue Smith
Editor: Rochelle Torke
Production Manager: Oriana Siska
Production Editor: Melissa Edeburn

Illustration © Clare Owen, 2019

Author photo courtesy Tim Sabatino/Theta Creata Studios

ISBN: Print 978-1-64152-437-7 | eBook 978-1-64152-438-4

Contents

Introduction
What Is Mindfulness, Anyway?

What Mindfulness Will Do for You

You've probably heard the term *mindfulness* and may wonder why it's popping up in so many places. Mindfulness is about being fully present and cultivating awareness of your surroundings and your actions. In this book, you will use it to train your brain not to be overly reactive to or overwhelmed by what is going on around us. You'll learn to become the boss of your mind and feelings.

Being mindful helps you step back, become present in the moment, and tap into your inner strength and resilience. In our modern world, teenagers like you are balancing a lot of potentially stressful things, like homework, sports, clubs, college applications, relationships, part-time jobs, and looking good on social media. If you ever feel tense or spread too thin, you're not alone.

The good news is that developing mindfulness will help you respond better to stress, improve your relationship with family and friends, and perform better in school. Mindfulness is a truly valuable skill that will serve you now as well as in the future. No matter how stressful things get, you'll be able to carry that peace and contentment with you wherever life takes you. That's what mindfulness is all about.

Building the Mindfulness Habit

I can hear you asking, "Do I have time for mindfulness?" The answer is yes. In fact, I believe you can't afford to skip mindfulness. My grandmother always told me, "In the time you were arguing, you could have been done."

Mindfulness can make a big difference in just 10 minutes of practice a day. By forming a valuable habit, you'll experience more personal benefits. The best kind of mindfulness is the kind that stays with you wherever you are—but first things first.

How Will This Book Help Me?

In *Mindfulness for Teens in 10 Minutes a Day*, you'll find four types of exercises:

CALMING EXERCISES to help you smooth out your mood in stressful times or unwind after a busy period.

FOCUSING EXERCISES to train your mind to concentrate with greater ease.

RECONNECTING EXERCISES that are feeling-centered to help you experience, identify, and accept a wide range of emotions. These exercises help you view emotions as information, not absolute truths. Emotions are like the weather—changing from time to time—and that is fine. These exercises will help you simply be with your emotions without reacting and judging.

RESPONDING EXERCISES to help you spot negative thoughts and emotions and steer your mind toward positive thoughts. These exercises prepare you to respond to challenging situations with greater ease and poise.

Each exercise includes a Go Deeper suggestion—a slight twist on the practice you just completed to connect more deeply to its benefits.

I encourage you to use a journal to keep track of the changes you notice and the benefits you observe. As you become more mindful, you'll find that writing in your journal is a great way to enhance your attention skills and reflect on your progress.

THE BENEFITS OF MINDFULNESS

Mindfulness has many benefits, but the two main ones that will be extremely valuable for you are better mood and increased attention and awareness.

Better mood: Practicing mindfulness for just 10 minutes a day can help you create and sustain feelings of peace, acceptance, lightheartedness, and ease. This routine prevents the mind from wandering toward negative thoughts, like excessive worry. You'll be able to reduce mood swings and handle complex situations with a clear head.

Increased attention and awareness: Mindfulness enhances your ability to focus. Daily mindful exercises draw your attention to a single thing—like your breath, a sound, or an object—to help your mind grow calmer and rest in the present moment. With increased concentration, your learning capacity will increase. Similarly, as mindfulness becomes a habit, you will be able to perform better under pressure, such as when taking a test, meeting new people, speaking in front of a group, or playing a sport.

Here are some other benefits of mindfulness:
- Improved fear management
- Deeper sleep
- Ease adapting to change
- Healthy eating habits
- Greater empathy
- Reduced risk of substance abuse

Where Do You Want to Start?

There's no one right way to begin the practice of mindfulness. This book presents exercises for every time of day to make it easy for you to find ones that fit your schedule. With one month of daily practice, you can make mindfulness a regular habit wherever you are. After all, the goal is to live more mindfully and to exist fully in the present moment at all times—not just when working on an exercise.

- Do you have trouble sleeping? A Calm exercise could be beneficial.
- Do you get anxious before tests? Perform a Focus activity.
- Are you procrastinating on a tough task? Consider doing a Reconnect exercise to understand the feelings that might be getting in your way.
- Want to be less reactive when someone annoys you? Try a Respond technique to cool down.

Your mindfulness practice will result in real improvement for you. Training your brain through mindfulness will give you benefits that will make a positive impact on your life. Simply by practicing mindfulness for 10 minutes every day, you will experience positive outcomes.

Breathing Techniques

Scientists have learned that how we *breathe* has a direct and powerful impact on how we *feel*. For example, a calming breath can help relax our parasympathetic system, allowing our bodies to relax. Stress hormones and blood pressure lower and our heart rate slows.

The way we breathe can activate the vagus nerve, which runs from our diaphragm to our brain, signaling the parasympathetic system to move us back into a calm state.

You don't have to be stressed out to gain benefits of breathing techniques. They are incredibly useful tools for increasing focus and achieving calm while practicing our mindfulness exercises. Throughout the book, we'll use the following types of breathing at the beginning of most exercises to make sure we are ready to engage. Use this section as a guide to performing the various breathing techniques.

4, 7, 8 BREATHING (YOGA BREATH)

I love 4, 7, 8 Breathing, or Yoga Breath, for several reasons. It is super relaxing, and you can use it anytime you feel stressed or are having a hard time falling asleep. It also very effectively helps lower cortisol (our main stress hormone) and puts the body in a fully relaxed state. Because you are breathing in a manner that draws your attention toward your breath, your anxiety will melt away.

1. Close your eyes and focus on your breathing in your diaphragm. As you deeply inhale down to your diaphragm, you will feel your belly rise. As you exhale, you will feel your belly lower.

2. Begin counting on the in-breath: Breathe in for a count of four (counting to yourself)—inhale, 2, 3, 4.

3. Hold for a count of seven (counting to yourself)—hold, 2, 3, 4, 5, 6, 7.

4. Exhale for a count of eight (counting to yourself)—exhale, 2, 3, 4, 5, 6, 7, 8.

5. Repeat this counting sequence four times, or the number of times indicated in each activity.

4 SQUARE BREATHING

4 Square Breathing is an excellent technique to use before doing something potentially stressful, such as taking a test, because it helps relax the body, which can improve your focus, improving your performance. This breathing technique is probably one of the easiest and quickest ways to calm the brain and bring you back into the present moment with an alert and stress-free mind. If possible, use this breathing technique for at least 8 minutes to maximize results.

Close your eyes and imagine a relaxing environment. My favorite place to imagine is the beach and ocean. As I inhale, I imagine the waves gently rolling up the beach. As I exhale, I imagine the waves rolling back out.

1. Find a comfortable position to sit, with both feet placed firmly on the ground.

2. Take a minute to notice your current body state and the pattern of your breathing.

3. Once you have settled into place and your starting point, place both hands either on your diaphragm (the area underneath your belly button) or, with palms up, resting on your thighs.

4. Slowly inhale for a count of four (counting to yourself)—inhale, 2, 3, 4. Notice your belly rise.

5. Hold for a count of four (counting to yourself)—hold, 2, 3, 4.

6. Slowly exhale for a count of four (counting to yourself)—exhale, 2, 3, 4. Notice your belly fall.

7. Hold for a count of four (counting to yourself)—hold, 2, 3, 4.

8. Repeat the exercise a minimum of four times.

2 + 4 BREATHING

If you need a quick energy boost, feel like you are coming down with a cold, or are becoming sleepy when you need to remain alert, try 2 + 4 Breathing.

Research shows that when we exhale for a longer period of time than we inhale, the immune system kicks into drive and our body becomes more alert. When powering through some homework, try this exercise to help you stay focused.

When using any breathing technique, keep your body fairly relaxed. One way to increase your body's relaxed state is to do this exercise lying on the floor. Place your right hand over your heart and the other hand over your diaphragm (the area underneath your belly button). Watch your hand fall as you exhale and rise as you fill your lungs with air. Practice 2 + 4 Breathing twice a day for 5 minutes during periods of high stress, such as finals week.

1. Find a comfortable position to sit, with both feet placed firmly on the ground.

2. Once you have settled into place, place both hands either on your diaphragm or, with palms up, resting on your thighs.

3. Slowly inhale for a count of two (counting to yourself)—inhale, 2. Notice your belly rise.

4. Hold for a count of two (counting to yourself)—hold, 2.

5. Slowly exhale for a count of four (counting to yourself)—exhale, 2, 3, 4. Notice your belly fall.

6. Hold for a count of two (counting to yourself)—hold, 2.

7. Repeat the exercise a minimum of 10 times.

Part I
Mindful Mornings

What Are Your Mornings Like?

Do you wake up feeling like a ray of sunlight, ready to shine on all who cross your path? Or do you just feel tired and irritable? Take a moment when you wake up to note how you feel. Observe your emotions without letting them overwhelm you. Pause and call up some reasons for gratitude as you greet the day. Focus on the day's potential, noting that you're strong enough to handle challenges and to uncover moments of contentment.

Remember to start your day with self-compassion rather than harsh words. For example, if you overslept, rather than getting upset at yourself, use a self-compassion statement like "Wow, I listened to my body and gave myself a little extra rest. Now, I need to get dressed and dive into the new day."

Starting your day with mindfulness can help clear your mind and create the opportunity to accept the day as it comes. I encourage you to try a new morning mindfulness exercise each weekday.

At the end of the month, evaluate which four exercises are your favorite for nonjudgmentally handling the day. Use those four exercises over the next two months as your go-to exercises. Use one exercise for a solid week. At the end of three months, you should find that your mornings feel brighter and that you're gliding into each day with greater enthusiasm. Now, let's go over some exercises to help you create some mindful mornings.

WHAT'S MOST IMPORTANT TO YOU?

Values describe who you need to be and what you need your life to be about. When you engage with your values, you are capable of accepting and moving through difficult challenges. Values do not need to be based on what you believe others expect of you. You have the power to choose values important to you.

Take a moment to consider the values that are important to you. Be willing to work at becoming the person you want to be and living the life you desire. Now, take a moment to commit to observing your behaviors and engaging in this book's exercises.

EXERCISE 1

Superhero Stance

TIME TO READ: 2 MINUTES   **TIME TO DO:** 8 MINUTES

Social psychologists have identified the concept of *power posing*. They note that how we hold our bodies and our posture influence how we think and feel about ourselves. Combining the power pose with a positive statement is a great way to connect to your internal strength and set powerful intentions for your day. Do this exercise on days when you have a big project or need to have a tough conversation with someone. Let the Superhero Stance help you draw on your inner strength.

1. Stand in front of a mirror, with your feet shoulder-width apart and your hands on your hips. Look yourself in the eyes while taking five deep breaths.

2. Say to yourself or out loud, "I seek strength, wisdom, and courage." Stand for 1 minute in this pose; look at yourself and hold these words to be true.

3. Say to yourself or out loud, "I find strength, wisdom, and courage." Stand for 1 minute in this pose; look at yourself and hold these words to be true.

4. Say to yourself or out loud, "I have strength, wisdom, and courage." Close your eyes and imagine yourself conquering the tasks of the day. Repeat this step again.

5. To finish, take five deep breaths.

GO DEEPER: At the end of each day, write in your journal about your accomplishments. After you finish, note the moments you showed strength, wisdom, or courage.

EXERCISE 2
Butterfly Hug

TIME TO READ: 3 MINUTES   **TIME TO DO:** 7 MINUTES

The Butterfly Hug exercise is a way to help calm your mind, connect to your inner strength, and experience loving-kindness toward yourself. A butterfly is a symbol of transformation. Starting this book is an example of your willingness to transform. You can do this exercise while lying in your bed, sitting on the edge of your bed, or sitting comfortably in a chair.

1.   With your body in a comfortable position, while in a quiet, private place, interlock your thumbs to create a butterfly shape (illustrated on page 5) and rest your palms on your chest, just below your collarbone.

2.   With your right hand, gently tap across your collarbone. Do the same with your left hand. Continue alternating between your left and right hands for one minute.

3.   Keeping your hands on your chest, take three deep breaths while saying to yourself or out loud, "May I be happy, healthy, and at ease."

4.   Repeat your butterfly tap, hug, and phrase three times.

5.   Finish the exercise by taking three deep breaths.

GO DEEPER: How did you feel? Did you notice how your mind shifted? Do you sense the inner strength to help you today? A great way to go deeper is to develop your own positive affirmation to use with the Butterfly Hug. Keep track of how your day goes with each positive affirmation you use.

EXERCISE 3
Mind the Mouth

TIME TO READ: 3 MINUTES   **TIME TO DO:** 7 MINUTES

Mindful eating is an easy way to practice your new skills—after all, you'll have at least three opportunities each day. There's no single way to eat mindfully. This exercise is about being aware of what you are eating and focusing on enjoying the moment. Eliminate other distractions, such as scrolling through social media, watching TV, or finishing homework. Rather, take a moment to look at, think about, smell, and savor your food.

1. Take three deep breaths. Place your food on your plate or in your bowl and look at it.

2. While taking three more deep breaths, think about the source of your food—the fields, farms, or ocean it came from.

3. Take three more deep breaths while thinking about the delicious smell.

4. Take three more deep breaths. Take a bite and notice the temperature, flavor, and texture of the food. As you chew, notice the sensations and the release of flavors in your mouth. As you swallow your food, note the sensations and the remaining flavors in your mouth.

5. After you finish the first bite, place your utensils down and take three deep breaths. Repeat the exercise until you are full.

6. Finish by taking three deep breaths.

GO DEEPER: Mindful eating is one of the easier habits to add to your day. I encourage you to extend the practice to include lunch and dinner. At the end of the day reflect for a moment: Did you notice improved focus for your day?

EXERCISE 4

Emotions in Motion

TIME TO READ: 3 MINUTES   **TIME TO DO:** 7 MINUTES

Emotions come from our mood, circumstances, and relationships with others. We label these feelings as good or bad. One technique for managing emotions is to acknowledge them and shift them in the opposite direction. Research has shown that smiling—even when we feel down—can help our body produce serotonin and dopamine, the happy hormones.

No matter how you feel emotionally, use this exercise to shift your feelings because—this is important to remember—*emotions are about how you feel about something and you can easily control them* using exercises like this one. This exercise will use 2 + 4 Breathing (page xiii).

1.   Close your eyes and take a moment to note your emotions.

2.   While doing 2 + 4 Breathing, notice where in your body the emotion is located and place your hands over that area.

3.   Smile and say to yourself or out loud, "I choose happiness." Repeat the phrase.

4.   While doing 2 + 4 Breathing again, smile and open your eyes. Notice the shift in your emotions. Repeat the phrase 10 times.

GO DEEPER: If you enjoy this exercise, end it by standing in front of a mirror while looking into your eyes. Smile at yourself and think about your ability to choose happiness. See whether you notice a difference in how you feel. If you prefer this option, do the exercise next time while looking at yourself in the mirror.

EXERCISE 5
Calm Breaths

TIME TO READ: 3 MINUTES   **TIME TO DO:** 7 MINUTES

Do you have a potentially stressful situation coming up? Maybe you have a big history test, or you had a fight with a friend and are worried about seeing them in school. Don't worry—this exercise will help you gain confidence and calm with mindful breathing.

1. In a quiet room, sit comfortably in a chair with your feet placed firmly on the ground. Gently rest your hands on your stomach. Set a timer for 7 minutes; use your phone if you don't have a timer handy.

2. Close your eyes and focus on your breathing. Breathe slowly until you can move the breath down to your belly. Place your hands on your stomach and feel it gently rise and fall.

3. While doing the 4, 7, 8 Breathing (Yoga Breath; page xi), say to yourself or out loud, "I can confidently take care of my day." Repeat three times.

4. Return to breathing normally, with eyes closed, until the timer completes.

GO DEEPER: If you liked this exercise, repeat it, but use the whole 10 minutes for the exercise. If you found this exercise challenging, consider using your mindfulness journal to explore why, by writing down a list of positive self-statements to reframe your experience.

EXERCISE 6
Soundscapes

TIME TO READ: 2 MINUTES   **TIME TO DO:** 8 MINUTES

This exercise will teach you how to focus your attention, how to harness it, and how to maintain it. Humans have an amazing capacity for focus, but that doesn't mean it comes naturally. That's why we need to train our attention to stay where we want it to for as long as we need it.

In this exercise, you are going to focus on one simple thing: sound. What do you hear around you? If you focus, you'll probably find that different sounds are going on all around you: indoor sounds, outdoor sounds, even the sounds inside your own body, like heartbeats and breaths and your stomach growling. In this activity, we are going to learn how to keep our attention focused on those sounds and not let it wander.

1. Sit comfortably in a chair with your feet placed firmly on the ground, or sit on the floor with your legs in Half Lotus (crisscrossed legs) position. Rest your hands on your knees or in your lap. Set your timer for 8 minutes.

2. Begin by focusing your attention on the sound of your breath flowing in and out. Start noticing other sounds around you. Let the various sounds arise, then be replaced by the next sound you notice.

3. Continue focusing only on sound. When your attention wanders, notice this, too, and gently bring it back to sound. Continue the exercise until your timer completes.

GO DEEPER: If you enjoy this exercise, try a version that incorporates physical sensations as well as sounds. For example, feel the carpet with your feet, or the texture of your clothes or another object in your hands. Let whatever arises in your soundscape or feeling-scape occupy your attention until it falls away.

EXERCISE 7

Monkey Moment

TIME TO READ: 2 MINUTES   **TIME TO DO:** 8 MINUTES

This exercise is a great technique for managing anxiety. Try imagining the anxiety inside you as a cute little monkey that worries about being left behind. Perhaps you could engage the monkey and have some compassion for its fears. Understand that you are much wiser than the monkey, so you can listen to its concerns and also choose how you feel about them.

1. Go to a favorite trail, a peaceful area, or simply take a walk in your neighborhood before you go to school. Set your timer for 8 minutes. Begin by walking slowly, placing one foot in front of the other—heel to toe.

2. While walking, repeat the positive self-mantra "May my monkey have peace."

3. As you say this, imagine the monkey calming down and resting on your back.

4. If your attention wanders, extend your mantra to the item bothering you. For example, if your sister has been bothering you lately, say, "May my sister have peace."

GO DEEPER: Consider drawing a picture in your journal of your anxiety monkey. Make it adorable and, almost, irresistible. Give your monkey a name. The next time you do this exercise, say, "Hey (name of monkey), I guess you are going along for a walk today." Use the same positive mantra, or one of your own. It could be something like "May I be kind. May I find rest. May I find joy."

RESPOND

EXERCISE 8
Connection Junction

TIME TO READ: 3 MINUTES   **TIME TO DO:** 7 MINUTES

Sometimes it's difficult to connect deeply with our emotions. The exercises in this book—like this one—were created to help you do just that. It is completely normal to feel overwhelmed by emotions. This exercise is about developing a way to sit calmly with all your emotions and not become consumed by them.

1. Find a comfortable position to meditate and set a timer for 7 minutes.

2. Begin by doing a round of 2 + 4 Breathing (page xiii). Slowly begin to notice your emotions, even if you can't identify them at first. Note where you feel them in your body. It could be tension in your back, or throbbing or lightness in your forehead, stomach, or chest.

3. When you note a sensation in your body, take a moment and say, "I feel . . ." and name the emotion.

4. Each time you say out loud, "I feel . . .," try to name the sensation in your body. Allow yourself to feel the feeling while releasing any negative aspects of the emotion.

5. End by repeating a round of 2 + 4 Breathing. Repeat the entire exercise four more times.

GO DEEPER: As you become more advanced in performing this exercise, try locating emotions for the full 10 minutes. Consider drawing or painting a picture of your emotions in your body. Over time, expand your emotional vocabulary beyond simple terms like sad, mad, or happy. This will help you become more in tune with your internal feelings.

EXERCISE 9
Daily Dose

TIME TO READ: 2 MINUTES   **TIME TO DO:** 8 MINUTES

A daily dose of meditation can help you enter a calm state. The best part about meditation is that it doesn't have to be difficult, and it can be quite pleasurable. The steps are simple, yet the rewards are great. Let your morning alarm be the signal to start your daily dose of calm.

1. Lie comfortably on your back in your bed. Notice your bed cradling your entire body. Place your hands over your diaphragm and begin to note the rise and fall of your belly as you breathe.

2. Imagine a clean black slate with just a small white dot in the center. Focus on the white dot.

3. While doing 2 + 4 Breathing (page xiii), bring your focus back to the clean black slate with the small white dot in the center. Focus on the white dot. Repeat four times.

4. While doing another round of 2 + 4 Breathing, draw your attention back to your bed, cradling your body. Imagine your body begging to become very light. Repeat four times.

5. While doing another round of 2 + 4 Breathing, draw your attention back to your body. Imagine your body cradled in warmth. Repeat four times.

6. Now, count backward, slowly, from 100. End the exercise with a final round of 2 + 4 Breathing.

GO DEEPER: If you experienced any unpleasant sensations during this exercise, write about them in your journal and then rip up the page. Take four deep breaths. Say to yourself or out loud, "I am at ease; I am at peace; I am calm; I am safe."

FOCUS

EXERCISE 10

If You See It, You Can Create It

TIME TO READ: 3 MINUTES   **TIME TO DO:** 7 MINUTES

Often athletes are taught to visualize their performance before competition. Many research studies have correlated how positive feelings and beliefs can positively affect performance. You can use visualization for yourself. For example, if you have a speech to give at school, visualize standing in front of the class; notice the students engaged in what you are saying. Confidently imagine how you remember all the talking points you have memorized. Notice how you speak in a calm, confident manner. Finish by imagining the class applauding at the end of your speech.

1. Set a timer for 7 minutes and get into a comfortable position.

2. Start the exercise with 2 + 4 Breathing (page xiii). Imagine a black room—so dark you cannot see your hand in front of your face.

3. Do another round of 2 + 4 Breathing. Imagine accomplishing your goal. Once you have imagined it, determine the steps to accomplish this goal.

4. Visualize it again, as if you are running a movie in your mind, seeing every action step completed to accomplish your goal. Note the sense of confidence you feel in completing the goal.

5. End the exercise with a final round of 2 + 4 Breathing. Repeat four times and then slowly open your eyes.

GO DEEPER: If you enjoy this exercise, repeat it at night instead of in the morning. Monitor your progress to determine which time of day may be best for this exercise. You could even write down your goals, the steps to achieve your goals, and the successful outcomes you reach. Writing the details down after you visualize them can embed a deeper sense of confidence and help you achieve success.

EXERCISE 11
Connect Four

TIME TO READ: 2 MINUTES   **TIME TO DO:** 8 MINUTES

I don't know about you, but Connect Four was one of my favorite games as a kid. Four seems to be a good number for the brain. This is why 4 Square Breathing (page xii) can be so calming. This exercise helps you reconnect to those feelings you avoid and allows you to move through them on a path of positivity.

1. Find a place to sit comfortably on the floor in a quiet room and set a timer for 8 minutes.

2. Focus your attention on your breath; if your mind wanders, bring it back to noticing your breath. Now, do a round of 4 Square Breathing.

3. Take a moment to find your inquisitive self. Scan your mind for awareness of unpleasant thoughts or emotions. Focus on these thoughts and emotions. Do another round of 4 Square Breathing.

4. Note the sensations arising in your body as you consider those unpleasant feelings or thoughts. Now, do another round of 4 Square Breathing.

5. Imagine a path lined with blue flowers and a bright light at the end of the path. Do another round of 4 Square Breathing.

6. Imagine entering the bright light at the end of the path and the sun warming your body. Now, do a final round of 4 Square Breathing.

GO DEEPER: Could you feel your body warm and relax at the end of the meditation? Draw a picture of the path in your journal. For the flowers, draw petals on the ground with the words of any unpleasant emotions you noticed. Next time, light a candle (in a safe place) or apply some lavender or spearmint essential oil to your wrist and use the whole 10 minutes for the meditation.

EXERCISE 12

Wise Grasshopper

TIME TO READ: 2 MINUTES   **TIME TO DO:** 8 MINUTES

Taking a moment to acknowledge and respond to our emotions can help us handle the day better. A wise mind can accept emotions. Learning to view feelings as just information, rather than pushing them away, can be liberating. Remember: No feeling lasts forever. Just as the happiest moment doesn't last forever, a moment of sadness or despair will subside as well. That is why mindfulness is important—it helps us remain wise.

1. Find a quiet place with room to stand and set a timer for 8 minutes.

2. Stand on your nondominant leg. Lift your dominant leg and bend it at your knee, standing so your raised ankle rests next to your standing knee. Bring together your palms, holding them at chest height in prayer position. Lift your shoulders and chest to stand still and upright. This is the Grasshopper stance.

3. Now, do a round of 4 Square Breathing (page xii). Say to yourself or out loud, "I am wise. I accept all emotions. I respond in wisdom."

4. Do another round of 4 Square Breathing. Note any pleasant or unpleasant emotions. Bring your attention back to your breathing. Continue to stand tall and still until the timer completes.

GO DEEPER: Were you able to hold the stance for the full 8 minutes? Write in your journal at the end of the exercise, noting how you handled all the emotions it brought up. Were you able to accept them and know they would pass?

CALM

EXERCISE 13

Morning Showers Bring Joy Flowers

TIME TO READ: 2 MINUTES   **TIME TO DO:** 8 MINUTES

This exercise is another meditation that can be integrated easily into one of your already established morning routines—out of this meditation, joy and happiness can spring. A calming shower can bring inspiration and wash away worry.

1. At the beginning of your morning shower, set your timer for 8 minutes. As you step in and begin to feel the warm water wash over your body, imagine the water washing away anxiety, stress, and worry.

2. Next, notice each area of your body touched by the water. Now, lather up a washcloth or sponge with a fragrant soap. Bring the cloth or sponge close to your nose. Inhale and smell the fragrance.

3. Begin to scrub every inch of your body. Imagine the soap scrubbing off all the stress of your life. Imagine fears, anger, worry, regrets, or any other unpleasant thoughts or feelings being scrubbed away by the soap and water. Now, rinse off all the soap.

4. Take four deep breaths. Say to yourself or out loud, "I am clean, fresh, free of worry—I am ready to start my day, distraction-free."

GO DEEPER: Are you refreshed and feeling a little more ready to handle the day? Next time, imagine that when you scrub your body you are energizing it for the day. Recognize power and confidence entering your body with the scrubbing. Create a positive self-mantra to use for an energizing, confidence-boosting shower. Take a moment to reflect on which resonates more with you—washing away worries or energizing your body with confidence.

EXERCISE 14

Laser Pointer

TIME TO READ: 2 MINUTES   **TIME TO DO:** 8 MINUTES

Concentration is an important skill, especially in our technology-fueled world where distractions are present constantly. In the past, people were content to sit in a park and observe, or sit in a restaurant and enjoy conversation without scrolling through their phone. Improving focus helps you become more confident, motivated, and thoughtful.

1. Sit comfortably on your bed with your legs crossed, if you are able. Set your timer for 8 minutes and pick a point in your room to focus on—maybe a picture on your wall or an object on your dresser. While focusing, start your 4, 7, 8 Breathing (Yoga Breath; page xi).

2. Place your palms together at heart height in prayer position. Imagine a string coming up out of your head lifting you to sit taller, pulling your shoulders slightly back and lifting your chest slightly. Again, focus your attention on the point in your room that you selected.

3. Next, do the 4, 7, 8 Breathing (Yoga Breath) again. Say to yourself or out loud, "I am focused. I am focused. I am focused."

4. Bring your attention back to the selected point in your room. Return to normal breathing until your timer completes. If you find your concentration drifting, nonjudgmentally pull your focus back to the selected point.

GO DEEPER: Do you feel focused? This week, put your phone down for several periods of 10 minutes each; focus your attention on the space around you and observe. Write in your journal about any changes in your ability to focus in class this week.

EXERCISE 15

Greet the Day Smiling

TIME TO READ: 2 MINUTES   **TIME TO DO:** 8 MINUTES

My mom always told me, "When you don't feel your best, try to look your best." Put on your favorite outfit and notice how quickly you feel better. The same can be said for smiling. Smiling has a scientifically proven effect on our mood. When we smile, it is like a party goes on in our mind—our brain produces the feel-good messengers dopamine, endorphins, and serotonin, which can transport us into a state of happiness and bliss. Next time you wake up feeling less than great, use this exercise to greet your day, bring happiness to yourself, and brighten your mood.

1. Go to the bathroom sink and turn on the warm water. Set a timer for 8 minutes.

2. While waiting for the water to warm, use 2 + 4 Breathing (page xiii). Look at yourself in the mirror and smile.

3. Place your hands in the warm water. Notice how it makes you feel. Look into the mirror and gently smile at yourself. Bring your awareness to your inner self. Turn off the water.

4. Place your warm hands on your cheeks while doing 2 + 4 Breathing.

5. Place a warm hand on your forehead and one on your belly while doing 2 + 4 Breathing.

6. Say to yourself or out loud, "I greet the day with happiness. May I fill others with happiness."

GO DEEPER: Make it your goal to help make one person happy today. Tonight, reflect on this topic while you write in your journal: What made you happy today? What did you do to bring happiness to someone else? Consider how dedicated you were to bringing yourself and others happiness by entering the day with this intention.

EXERCISE 16

Heart of Happiness

TIME TO READ: 2 MINUTES   **TIME TO DO:** 8 MINUTES

Sometimes it's hard to appreciate every moment of every day. It is important to learn how to focus on pleasant moments and positive emotions, even on a hectic or turbulent day. You can teach your mind to notice the high points, even if they aren't as plentiful as usual that day. When you connect to your heart in the present, you can cultivate more joy, happiness, and fulfillment during your day—no matter what challenges the day presents.

1. While standing in your room, set a timer for 8 minutes.

2. Start the exercise with 2 + 4 Breathing (page xiii) and begin walking slowly through your room or look through your closet observing and appreciating the many items you have. Recall the moments these items came into your room. Take note of the feeling of satisfaction or joy each item brings.

3. While doing another round of 2 + 4 Breathing, pick up an item that you feel a spark of joy from and say to yourself or out loud, "Thank you for the joy you bring."

4. Repeat with other items until the timer runs out.

GO DEEPER: Take a moment to reflect on your pleasant emotions. Do you feel happy? Consider writing in your journal about the items that bring joy and happiness into your room or write a note of gratitude to someone who gave you an item that still brings you joy.

EXERCISE 17
My Favorite Things

TIME TO READ: 2 MINUTES   **TIME TO DO:** 8 MINUTES

Do you remember your favorite stuffed animal or blanket that brought you comfort when you were a child? Our favorite things tend to have a calming effect on us. This exercise is for those moments when our mind is racing. You will see that simply listing your favorite things will have a calming effect.

1. Find a comfortable place to sit or lie in your room and set a timer for 8 minutes.

2. Start the exercise with 2 + 4 Breathing (page xiii). Say to yourself or out loud your favorite four movies, TV shows, books, or songs.

3. Do 2 + 4 Breathing again. Say to yourself or out loud your favorite four animals.

4. Do 2 + 4 Breathing again. Say to yourself or out loud your favorite four colors.

5. Do 2 + 4 Breathing again. Say to yourself or out loud your favorite four memories.

6. Do 2 + 4 Breathing one final time. Bring your attention to normal breathing until your timer completes.

GO DEEPER: After the exercise, take a moment to write in your journal. Write down as many details of each favorite thing as you can. Consider creating a vision board of your favorite items to keep in your room. On days when you feel anxious, sit and look at the vision board and breathe until you feel calm and grounded.

EXERCISE 18
Fire Beads

TIME TO READ: 2 MINUTES   **TIME TO DO:** 8 MINUTES

Do you ever wake up in a fog and have a hard time focusing on what you need to do first? This exercise will focus your attention, energize you, and connect you to the present. You will need a string of beads for this exercise. In this exercise, you will use Fire Breath. This breathing exercise wasn't described in the Breathing section (page x), so it is new and might take a couple tries to master. Don't worry—you are learning another technique that will bring you mindfulness.

1. Sit comfortably on the floor in Half Lotus (crisscrossed legs) position.

2. Hold a string of beads in front of you at eye height between the thumb and index finger of your right hand. Roll a bead quickly between your thumb and index finger. Relax your stomach. Keep your mouth closed.

3. Take a quick, shallow inhale through your nose and exhale quickly through your nose. Breathe rapidly for a count of 10 inhales. Pump your belly button in and out as you breathe.

4. Place the string of beads between your palms at eye height. Quickly roll the beads back and forth in your palms. Relax your stomach. Keep your mouth closed. Repeat the breathing technique in step 3.

5. Hold the string of beads in front of you at eye height between the thumb and index finger of your left hand. Roll a bead quickly between your thumb and index finger. Relax your stomach. Keep your mouth closed. Repeat the breathing technique in step 3.

6. Slow your breath. Place the beads between the thumb and index finger of your preferred hand. Take one inhale breath as you roll your thumb and index finger around one bead. Move to the next bead and exhale one breath as you slowly roll your thumb and index finger around one bead. Move your way through all the beads, inhaling and exhaling.

GO DEEPER: Perform the exercise outside and notice how nature enhances it. Does your focus lessen or intensify when you add nature to the experience?

EXERCISE 19
Gut Feelings

TIME TO READ: 3 MINUTES   **TIME TO DO:** 7 MINUTES

Our brain makes decisions by combining logic and critical thinking with our emotions. Learning when to trust our gut feelings is important. It is like following GPS when we are driving—it can take us down the right path. This exercise is about helping us understand our gut feelings and becoming more in touch with them.

1. Set a timer for 7 minutes. Lie on your bed, really sinking into it.

2. Start the exercise with 4, 7, 8 Breathing (Yoga Breath; page xi). Bring to mind a recent situation or issue of resistance or procrastination. Enter the situation. Notice any sensation that arises in your body. Notice whether there is a place in your body where "no" resides. Notice any colors, textures, or words that represent the feelings in your body.

3. Continue to stay in this experience and use the 4, 7, 8 Breathing (Yoga Breath) again. Now, release the negativity of the experience. Visualize a black wall and bring to mind a time you said yes and completed the task on time. Enter into your experience. Notice any sensation that arises in the body. Notice any colors, textures, or words that represent the feelings in your body.

4. Nod your head four times in agreement, acknowledging where in your body this feeling resides. Continue to stay in this experience and use the 4, 7, 8 Breathing (Yoga Breath). Notice how your body tells you so much and provides insight. Place your palms together at the center of your heart. Nod one more time, telling your body thank you.

5. Return to normal breathing until the timer completes.

GO DEEPER: Write in your journal the feelings you noticed and how they felt in your body. Talk to another person about your gut feelings and have them share about theirs. Track, over time, in your journal whether your gut feelings pan out. Evaluate your relationship to your "gut feelings" and what they tell you.

EXERCISE 20
Catch and Release

TIME TO READ: 2 MINUTES   **TIME TO DO:** 8 MINUTES

Have you ever done catch-and-release fishing? You can take a similar approach with unpleasant feelings. Take a moment to experience and acknowledge an unpleasant or uncomfortable feeling. Then you can release the emotion to help you tolerate and transform the feeling rather than respond negatively to it. Use the acronym FISH (find, identify, summon, hold) to recognize and release unpleasant feelings.

1. Set a timer for 8 minutes and lie comfortably on your bed with your hands gently resting over your belly button.

2. Start the exercise with 2 + 4 Breathing (page xiii).

3. **F:** Find an unpleasant or uncomfortable feeling.

4. **I:** Identify where you feel the uncomfortable feeling in your body.

5. **S:** Summon the experience that brought on the feeling. Did you argue with your parents last night? Did your sister or brother wake you up rudely? Are you worried about something today?

6. **H:** Hold the feeling in your body for a moment. Now, imagine throwing the feeling back into a river and watching it swim away.

7. Repeat 2 + 4 Breathing. Take a moment to breathe in the peaceful calm of the gently flowing river.

8. Repeat 2 + 4 Breathing. Continue until the timer completes.

GO DEEPER: If you are experiencing deeper suffering with your feelings and thoughts, take a moment to write these questions in your journal: What are you silently suffering? Who are two people you can talk to today to gain some support and understanding? What unfairness do you feel you have to endure? What action can you take today to let go of the unfairness and heal? Repeat to yourself or out loud four times, "I will not let my suffering and unpleasant feelings keep me stuck."

Part II
Midday Mindfulness

What Are Your Days Like?

We receive many benefits from engaging in mindfulness. Utilizing magnetic resonance imaging (MRI), Harvard University researchers found that mindfulness increased general mental aptitude. More importantly, they found that meditation and mindfulness had a profound impact on the electrical activity within the brain to produce a calming effect. Participants who meditated or utilized mindfulness skills daily reported a reduction in general tension, anxiety, and irritability.

Take a moment to assess how your day is going. It is natural to feel out of sorts as the day progresses. Use this next set of exercises to energize yourself. They will help you thrive and stay focused, even during your busiest days.

WHERE DO YOU WANT TO MAKE A CHANGE?

You have a choice to change your feelings and surroundings. Decide on the life you want to live and commit to building the mindfulness habit. Learn to respond to your unpleasant thoughts and feelings just by acknowledging their existence. Take time to identify pleasant thoughts and feelings on a more regular basis. As you learn to respond differently to unpleasant thoughts and feelings, you'll find that they control you less and less.

The following exercises will help you understand that mindfulness is about choice—the choice to feel what you want to feel. You have a choice to acknowledge all your feelings and you have a choice about how they affect you.

EXERCISE 21
PETS

TIME TO READ: 2 MINUTES   **TIME TO DO:** 8 MINUTES

Pets bring joy and happiness and help us relax during moments of high stress. During days at school when you feel exceptionally stressed or overwhelmed, take a PETS (push, emotions, thoughts, sensations) break. A wise mind develops skills to distract itself from unpleasant thoughts or feelings. This exercise will help you move into a calm state.

1. During your break or lunch, set your timer for 8 minutes and walk around the campus or break area.

2. Start the exercise with 2 + 4 Breathing (page xiii).

3. **P:** Push away your problems for this time. Imagine locking up that worrisome thought in a locker. Shut the door on your problem for now. Of course, use your best judgment. If your problem, or the source of your worry, can't be addressed right this minute, then thinking about it too much is just draining your energy for the present moment. Instead, say to yourself or out loud, "This is a problem for later or tomorrow."

4. **E:** Emotions are influenced by actions. Take a moment to change what you're doing (your actions) to create a shift in your feelings and mood.

5. **T:** Thoughts matter. Focus your thoughts on something positive to lift a depressed or anxious mood. Think about something you are looking forward to this weekend to relieve stress.

6. **S:** Sensations can distract your mind from unpleasant feelings or thoughts. Suck on a piece of candy, chew a piece of gum, or inhale a pleasant smell.

7. Once again, remind yourself that your worries are locked up in your locker until the end of the day.

8. Finish the exercise with 2 + 4 Breathing. Notice the calm wash over your thoughts and feelings.

GO DEEPER: Do this exercise again as you head home today. Push the worries and stresses into an imaginary box that you carry home so they cannot affect you. Place the box on a shelf when you get home. That's the best part of this exercise: You can keep the box on the shelf or—as you advance in your mindfulness pursuit—you can open the box and work with the experiences that are inside.

FOCUS

EXERCISE 22
What's the Object?

TIME TO READ: 3 MINUTES   **TIME TO DO:** 7 MINUTES

Are there moments when you find you have become lost in your thoughts? One technique to help improve our focus and concentration is utilizing object meditation. An object meditation redirects your mind to notice the details of an object. Learning this technique can help increase the capacity to focus and concentrate on the present. For this exercise, use any object in your surroundings. Ideally, you want to pick something easily within your view and something with different textures and features.

1. Find a quiet place and set your timer for 7 minutes. Do a round of 4 Square Breathing (page xii) and take a moment to direct your focus onto the object you have selected. Take a moment to focus on the object.

2. Take another moment to notice the features of the object.

3. Notice whether the object is smooth or rough. Does it have ridges or indentations? Is the object hard or soft? Notice how the light hits the object. Notice whether the object is solid or transparent.

4. Take a moment and connect again to your breathing with another round of 4 Square Breathing. Repeat three times, or until the timer completes.

GO DEEPER: Were you surprised about how many details you were able to identify? If you don't have access to an object, use visualization. For example, visualize standing on top of a mountain and looking at the night sky. Notice how bright the stars and moon appear with less light pollution from the city to dim them. Think about the light emanating from the moon and stars. Notice a sense of calm and stillness as you visualize the night sky. Think about the dark space around each star.

EXERCISE 23

Embracing the Good, the Bad, and the Ugly

TIME TO READ: 3 MINUTES   **TIME TO DO:** 7 MINUTES

Emotions are not simply good or bad; they exist on a spectrum. When you ignore, push away, or run away from emotions you might label as "bad," you deny parts of yourself. When you take a moment to look at so-called bad emotions, you will find they are not so bad after all. In a sense, you learn to have compassion for unpleasant emotions and realize they are just clues to help you process the world. Take a few moments to connect to the emotions you might be pushing away in this exercise.

1. Set a timer for 7 minutes and find a quiet place to sit with both feet placed firmly on the ground. Close your eyes and start your 4 Square Breathing (page xii).

2. Bring to mind an unpleasant emotion you are experiencing today. It could be anxiety, worry, concern, or sadness. With your next inhale, imagine embracing the unpleasant emotion and visualize sucking it up, like a vacuum sucking up dirt.

3. Continue your breathing exercise and realize that everyone on this planet has felt this unpleasant emotion at one time or another. Your intention in inhaling this emotion is to acknowledge it and take it out of your immediate space. Imagine that by inhaling the emotion you are helping the world and your day become a little freer from reacting to that unpleasant emotion.

4. Now, exhale and imagine breathing out pleasant emotions, such as joy, happiness, peace, kindness, or relief. Visualize the space around you filling with these pleasant emotions, almost like a warm pink cloud.

5. Repeat the 4 Square Breathing exercise four more times while inhaling unpleasant emotions and exhaling pleasant emotions in their place.

GO DEEPER: Take a moment to consider what you noticed. If you found that your chest became tight, take a moment to visualize your lungs and heart enlarging to be able to hold the unpleasant emotions, almost like a nursery—a place for the unpleasant emotions to experience love and kindness. Are you able to accept the unpleasant emotions a little easier now? Consider painting a picture representing the unpleasant emotions and some kindness and compassion and increasing pleasant emotions around you. Your painting could be abstract with just colors on a canvas.

EXERCISE 24

Notifications That Matter

TIME TO READ: 2 MINUTES   **TIME TO DO:** 8 MINUTES

In our modern world, our cell phones are constantly making noise. The minute you hear that notification on your phone, it distracts you from the world around you. You might even constantly open your apps to check responses to your social media posts. Our mind has become programmed to think that these notifications matter, but, often, they can leave us stressed and depressed. How often have you looked at messages only to find they were left unread or noticed that few followers liked a post or viewed your latest story? The notifications that matter are your feelings. Feelings provide information. Sometimes we need to STOP and pay attention.

1. Set a timer for 8 minutes and find a quiet place to sit with both feet placed firmly on the ground.

2. **S:** Stop your thoughts; essentially, put them on pause.

3. **T:** Take time to breathe, using 2 + 4 Breathing (page xiii).

4. **O:** Observe your surroundings. What are five things you see? What are four things you can touch? What are three things you hear? What are two things you smell? What is one thing you can taste?

5. **P:** Proceed with considering how you feel in the moment about your thoughts. Make appropriate choices and decisions based on your thoughts and feelings.

6. Bring your attention back to your breath and start another round of 2 + 4 Breathing.

7. **S:** Smile.

8. **T:** Take time to breathe, using 2 + 4 Breathing.

9. **O:** Open yourself to feel deeply in the moment.

10. **P:** Praise yourself for taking this moment to connect to your feelings.

11. Bring your attention back to your breath and end with a final round of 2 + 4 Breathing.

GO DEEPER: Ask a friend to do this exercise with you. Talk with them about the benefits you both experience at the end of the week.

EXERCISE 25

Self-Care-Ation

TIME TO READ: 3 MINUTES   **TIME TO DO:** 7 MINUTES

Self-care is about taking a mini vacation from your worries and stresses. This one takes a little preparation, but it is worth the time. Take a zipper-lock bag and fill it with a combination of these items: flavored lip balm, mints, gum, lollipops, lavender essential oil, spearmint essential oil, scented lotion, or any scented body care item. Keep this kit in your purse, bag, or backpack. On those days you feel a little stressed, it's time for a Self-Care-Ation.

1. Find a quiet place to sit or walk and set a timer for 7 minutes. Pick a mint, piece of gum, or a lollipop from your self-care-ation kit and start your 4, 7, 8 Breathing (Yoga Breath; page xi).

2. Look at your treat. Slowly remove any wrapper, if needed. Notice the sound, color, shape, and density of your treat. Smell your treat and notice any fragrance. Place the treat in your mouth. Notice the flavors. Roll the treat around in your mouth. Notice its sensations and textures.

3. Next, select a body care item and start another round of 4, 7, 8 Breathing (Yoga Breath). Open your body care item. Hold the item near enough to smell it. Notice any fragrance. Apply the body care item to your body. Notice

the sensation as you apply the item. Notice any changes to your skin or lips as you apply it. Notice the smells once you apply the body care item. Take a moment to deeply breathe in the fragrance.

4. Finish with one final round of 4, 7, 8 Breathing (Yoga Breath).

GO DEEPER: Are you relaxed? Do you feel like you took a mini vacation? Next time, at the end of the exercise, close your eyes and imagine a relaxing environment; it can be some real place you have been, or some place you have seen in a movie or magazine, or read about in a book. You could also do this exercise while taking a bath.

FOCUS

EXERCISE 26
Name Game

TIME TO READ: 2 MINUTES   **TIME TO DO:** 8 MINUTES

When getting ready to take a pop quiz or test, do you feel as though your mind has gone blank? In those moments, pulling yourself back into the present is essential to help you focus. The Name Game is a great exercise to get your mind back into the present and focused on the now. When we access the part of our memory that recalls the names of objects, we can calm the anxious mind and increase our attention and focus.

1. Set a timer for 8 minutes and sit upright in a chair or outside in a quiet place, with both feet placed firmly on the ground.

2. Start the exercise with 2 + 4 Breathing (page xiii). Look in front of you and scan the space clockwise, naming every object you see.

3. Now, look counterclockwise and, again, name every object you see.

4. Repeat steps 2 and 3 until your timer completes.

5. End the exercise with 2 + 4 Breathing.

GO DEEPER: Did you notice you were able to focus after the exercise? Next time, touch and name objects on your desk. Sometimes engaging in a sensory experience can help ground us in the present.

EXERCISE 27
Serenity Stand, Thankful Tuck

TIME TO READ: 2 MINUTES   **TIME TO DO:** 8 MINUTES

During a long day at school or work, it can be a good practice to take a moment of serenity. It can help bring your body back into a calm state. Also, taking a moment to thank your body for serving you well can help lower stress.

1. Set your timer for 8 minutes and stand with your arms lifted toward the sky. Feel your body elongate, as if a string is pulling you taller. Imagine the sunlight entering your fingertips and warming your body. Start your 4, 7, 8 Breathing (Yoga Breath; page xi).

2. Now, lengthen your spine, roll your arms like you are going to dive into a pool, tuck your chin to your chest, and roll down to touch your toes. Bring your attention to your feet. Thank your feet for carrying you through the day. Slowly begin to roll back up to a standing position. As you unroll each area of your body, take a moment to show gratitude to each part of your body for serving you well today.

3. Repeat the entire exercise two more times.

4. End with a final round of 4, 7, 8 Breathing (Yoga Breath).

GO DEEPER: Being thankful can activate the positive emotion center of our brain. Write down 10 things you are grateful for today on different Post-it Notes. Scatter these around your room or in your locker to consider in those moments when you don't feel your best. As you read them, take a deep breath and allow your body to move into a calm, relaxed state.

EXERCISE 28

Show Me the LOVE

TIME TO READ: 3 MINUTES   **TIME TO DO:** 7 MINUTES

Do you ever find you are your worst critic? It is amazing how easily self-talk can become critical and harsh. That is why self-love is an important act to learn. The acronym LOVE can help. When you find yourself talking negatively about your thoughts, actions, and emotions, remember to stop and LOVE (listen, observe, validate, evaluate/energize). You might find your thoughts, actions, and emotions have some validity and can provide good information, but it is important to use them in a loving way toward yourself.

1. Find a quiet place to sit comfortably with both feet placed firmly on the ground, and set your timer for 7 minutes. Rest your hands on your thighs, palms up. Begin with 4, 7, 8 Breathing (Yoga Breath; page xi).

2. **L:** Listen to your thoughts.

3. **O:** Observe how you acted in response to those thoughts.

4. **V:** Validate your experience.

5. **E:** Evaluate your options for response.

6. Start another round of 4, 7, 8 Breathing (Yoga Breath).

7. **L:** Listen to your emotions.

8. **O:** Observe your response to your emotions.

9. **V:** Validate your experience.

10. **E:** Energize yourself for action—determine the action you will take on these emotions, feelings, and thoughts for the day.

11. End with a final round of 4, 7, 8 Breathing (Yoga Breath).

GO DEEPER: If you enjoy this exercise, tonight, write a love letter to yourself. Acknowledge all the wonderful things about you. Note in the letter how you handled your day positively, including thoughts, feelings, and behaviors.

EXERCISE 29
Surf

TIME TO READ: 2 MINUTES   **TIME TO DO:** 8 MINUTES

It is helpful to think of our emotions as surf on the beach.
There are times we allow our feelings to wash over us. In these
moments, it is time to respond with a surfing mind. You can
learn to surf with the feelings rather than letting them overwhelm you. If your mind wanders during this exercise, it is
okay. Take a moment to note your wandering mind and get
back into the exercise.

1. Set your timer for 8 minutes. Sit comfortably and place
    your attention on your body. The goal is not to relax, but,
    rather, increase the awareness of your feelings and your
    body sensations.

2. Close your eyes and start your 4 Square Breathing
    (page xii). Notice your body's posture. Notice how your
    body fills with oxygen that gives energy to your muscles.
    Wiggle your toes.

3. Imagine your breath can surf across your body and provide
    energy to every muscle. Imagine your breath traveling to
    your right hand. Notice the sensations in the tips of your
    fingers as your breath rises and falls. Take a moment of
    gratitude for your fingers that help you grasp and hold
    objects. Now, surf your breath across your body to your

feet and ankles. Notice the sensations. Take a moment of gratitude for your feet and ankles that help you move and change direction. Now, surf your breath to the other areas of your body and share a moment of gratitude.

4. When finished, take a moment to say to yourself or out loud, "Thank you, body; thank you for the feelings we feel."

5. Close the exercise with a round of 4 Square Breathing.

GO DEEPER: Consider drawing a wave in your journal today and writing on the crest of the wave the feelings you noticed during the exercise. Write under the wave, "I can ride through my feelings; they won't pull me down and stop me."

EXERCISE 30
Hello Moments

TIME TO READ: 2 MINUTES   **TIME TO DO:** 8 MINUTES

Do you have moments during the day when your mind is prone to wander? I call these Hello Moments. In those moments our minds might drift to the past or the future. It is during these times that we want to pull our attention back to the present. This exercise will help you do just that.

1. Set your timer for 8 minutes and find a quiet place to sit or stand. Notice where your thoughts were just a moment ago. Were they in the past, present, or future? Start with 2 + 4 Breathing (page xiii).

2. Bring yourself to the present moment and say hello to yourself. Do another round of 2 + 4 Breathing.

3. Bring yourself to the present moment and say to yourself or out loud, "Focus on now. Focus on today." Do another round of 2 + 4 Breathing.

4. Return to what you were doing. Say hello to the task. Ask yourself what you need to do right now.

GO DEEPER: Next time, before starting the activity, take a moment to say to yourself or out loud, "Be patient. Be kind." Then take four deep breaths. When finished with the activity, reflect: Were you patient and kind to yourself? Did you notice anything in particular about how you feel about yourself at this moment? Write these answers and other thoughts in your journal.

EXERCISE 31

Eat the Frog

TIME TO READ: 2 MINUTES   **TIME TO DO:** 8 MINUTES

"Eat the frog first," shorthand for advice attributed to Mark Twain, is another way of saying that if you have an important or unde- sirable task, it's best to tackle it first. What are the frogs in your life? This exercise will help you address them immediately during your day or when you get home from school.

1. Find a quiet, comfortable place to sit and set your timer for 8 minutes. Start the exercise with your 4 Square Breathing (page xii). Imagine a light streaming down from the sky, providing you with energy and clarity. Consider the tasks you need to complete today and notice any sensations in your body as you consider each task.

2. Do another round of 4 Square Breathing. Imagine the light illuminating what you have been avoiding. Imagine the light providing the energy needed to take care of this task.

3. Do another round of 4 Square Breathing. Notice the feeling of satisfaction you have from taking care of the task you have been avoiding.

4. Finish the exercise with one more round of 4 Square Breathing.

GO DEEPER: Were you able to think of the task you are avoiding? Could you feel the sense of energy the light provided? Next time you use this exercise, listen to some energetic music and continue to listen to the music as you complete the task.

EXERCISE 32
Lily Pads

TIME TO READ: 2 MINUTES   **TIME TO DO:** 8 MINUTES

It is easy for our days to feel unbalanced. We feel overwhelmed and this can stop us from completing our tasks. This exercise is an effective way to feel centered, even during our craziest days. Imagine a frog sitting on a lily pad with hungry little fish swimming around in the pond beneath him. If the frog stays centered on the lily pad, he can happily catch and eat the bugs. Think of the bugs as your feelings. Take in the moments around you. Watch how happiness can be caught.

1. Find a comfortable place outside and set your timer for 8 minutes. Sit comfortably on the ground in the Half Lotus (crisscrossed legs) position.

2. Start the exercise with your 4 Square Breathing (page xii). Think about happy moments this past month. Think about a silly video you watched on YouTube. Think about a funny joke. Notice the happy feelings starting to surround you.

3. Do 4 Square Breathing again. Imagine you are a frog on a lily pad. Catch the feelings and imagine sucking them into your mouth to eat. Notice the sensations in your body as you pull the feelings into your mouth.

4. Do 4 Square Breathing again. Smile to yourself and say to yourself or out loud, "I am as happy as a frog croaking on a lily pad with a full belly."

GO DEEPER: Consider drawing a picture of your frog. Draw positive-feeling words above the frog and put little wings on the words, like they are feeling bugs. Put your picture in the area where you do your homework. When you feel stressed or overwhelmed by homework, look at your frog and smile.

EXERCISE 33

Clouds

TIME TO READ: 2 MINUTES   **TIME TO DO:** 8 MINUTES

Thoughts and emotions can cloud the mind, which can decrease concentration and the ability to focus. Taking a mindful moment at the end of your school day can help improve concentration and increase a sense of calm. A focused mind will help you handle the remainder of the day.

1. Find a comfortable place to sit outside and set a timer for 8 minutes. Look up at the sky. Bring yourself into this moment. Become aware of your breath by starting your 2 + 4 Breathing (page xiii).

2. Whatever your thoughts or feelings might be, take a moment to acknowledge them and allow them to be. Don't judge or analyze—just let them be. Imagine them as clouds in the sky. Take your focus off these thoughts and feelings for a moment. With each exhalation, imagine the clouds of your mind are blown away.

3. Do another round of 2 + 4 Breathing. Be fully present with your breath. Concentrate on your breath. Now, shift your focus from your breath to any sensations in your body. Just acknowledge the sensations without judgment or analysis. If thoughts or emotions try to invade, acknowledge them and imagine them as clouds. Focus your exhalation in a manner that blows these clouds away.

4. Do another round of 2 + 4 Breathing. Be fully present with your breath. Imagine you are lying in a field watching clouds, or if there are clouds in the sky where you are, notice their shapes. Notice how they change shape as they float. Again, visualize your thoughts and emotions as clouds. Notice how thoughts and emotions form and change. Once again, focus your exhalation in a manner that blows these clouds away.

5. Finish the exercise with one final round of 2 + 4 Breathing.

GO DEEPER: Take a moment to set your intention before the activity—consider what you would like to notice after completing the activity—increased focus, a sense of calm, or increased positive emotions. Repeat the exercise both with and without intention setting. After doing it both ways, take a moment to reflect: Did you notice something different from when you first practiced this activity?

EXERCISE 34

Check It Before You Wreck It

TIME TO READ: 2 MINUTES   **TIME TO DO:** 8 MINUTES

Ever heard the expression "Check yourself before you wreck yourself"? This saying holds some wisdom we can mindfully apply to our mindfulness training. Ever find yourself stumbling down the hall or running into things? We can sometimes walk through life without focused attention. Take a moment to do this exercise to help you become more fully aware of your body.

1. Set your timer for 8 minutes and sit comfortably with both feet placed firmly on the ground. Start with 4, 7, 8 Breathing (Yoga Breath; page xi). Squeeze your hands as tightly as you can; notice the sensations as you squeeze your hands. Release your hands; notice the sensations as you release your hands. Look at your left palm. Notice the lines in your palm. Trace the lines of your palm with your finger.

2. Do another round of 4, 7, 8 Breathing (Yoga Breath). Look at your right palm. Notice the lines in your palm. Trace the lines of your palm with your finger.

3. Do another round of 4, 7, 8 Breathing (Yoga Breath). Take a moment to curl your toes; notice the sensations as you curl your toes. Move your legs forward in front of you, pointing

your toes; notice the sensations as you point your toes. Rock back on your heels and flex your feet, pulling your toes up toward the sky; notice the sensations as you pull up your toes.

4. End the exercise with one last round of 4, 7, 8 Breathing (Yoga Breath).

GO DEEPER: You can extend this exercise by adding some awareness language. For example, as you point your toes, say to yourself or out loud, "I am becoming aware of my right toes. I notice my big toe and my pinky. I can wiggle my big toe. I am aware of my toenail on my big toe. I can feel the soles of my feet as they rest on the ground."

EXERCISE 35

SAFE

TIME TO READ: 2 MINUTES   **TIME TO DO:** 8 MINUTES

Cultivating a positive mood, one of kindness and compassion, is one of the benefits of mindfulness meditation. This exercise can be helpful midday to help increase positive emotions. Other benefits include silencing your internal critic, strengthening your ability to show empathy, and an increased sense of social connection.

1. Find a comfortable place to sit, either outside or inside, and set your timer for 8 minutes. Sit in a Half Lotus (crisscrossed legs) position and start with 2 + 4 Breathing (page xiii).

2. **S:** Sense what pleasant feelings you notice. Lift your chest slightly and breathe in the pleasant feelings. Breathe out any unpleasant feelings.

3. **A:** Allow the pleasant feelings to swirl inside you and fill your lungs as you breathe in. Allow the unpleasant feelings to float away as you breathe them out.

4. **F:** Feel the emotions building within you. Ask yourself, "What do I need?" For example, if you have been critical of yourself, recognize you need kindness and compassion. Say, "May I know kindness and compassion."

5. **E:** Expand your awareness of your feelings with each breath. Expand your feelings to those around you by saying, "May we all know kindness and compassion."

6. End with a round of 2 + 4 Breathing.

GO DEEPER: Do you notice any shift in your positive mood state? Vary the positive mood state affirmation for steps 4 and 5 each time you practice this meditation. Encourage a friend or classmate to join you to practice this midday meditation. Does this change your experience? Ask your classmate about any benefits they noticed.

EXERCISE 36

Bubble

TIME TO READ: 2 MINUTES   **TIME TO DO:** 8 MINUTES

Do you ever regret the choices you have made? Do you struggle with frustrations over your circumstances? Learning to accept and respond to where we are at this moment is an important process. This activity can help you find an appreciation for your experiences.

1. Find a comfortable place to sit or lie and set a timer for 8 minutes. Begin the exercise with a round of 4, 7, 8 Breathing (Yoga Breath; page xi).

2. Imagine a bubble sitting in the palm of your hand. Notice the round shape and the clarity of the bubble. Notice that the bubble is strong—that you can push on the bubble and it doesn't pop. Feel the bubble as a secure place—one that cannot blow away. Watch the bubble grow larger than you. Sense the warmth from your heart fill the bubble. Take a deep inhale and imagine moving inside the bubble. Imagine the bubble as a clean, safe space.

3. This bubble will keep you safe as you travel through time to answer the question "How did I get here?" Nothing bad will happen to you in this bubble; you are safe, and no one will know you are here. Imagine that the bubble transports you into the sky. You can watch all that is going on around

you as you fly inside your bubble—up into the sky. Feel how freeing it is to be up this high without any fear, knowing you are safe inside your bubble.

4.   Pause. Look all around yourself and accept the world around you. Accept that this is where you are right now in your life. Accept the things you have experienced in your life—relationships, decisions, things you have learned, things you have lost, the moments of happiness and sadness. All of it brought you here. Notice a sense of peace and contentment. Everything that has happened has had a reason and a purpose.

5.   End the exercise with a round of 4, 7, 8 Breathing (Yoga Breath).

GO DEEPER: Could you feel the warmth and safety? Do you feel like you can be more accepting of your experiences? Consider some positive affirmations you might pair with this exercise. Write them down and, next time, reflect on those affirmations after completing this activity.

EXERCISE 37
Giant Growing

TIME TO READ: 2 MINUTES   **TIME TO DO:** 8 MINUTES

Your mind is constantly growing and maturing. MRI studies have found that individuals can expand their neural brain mass in both the long- and short-term memory centers through mindfulness and meditation. Mindfulness helps you grow and pay attention to your wise mind. Midday is a great time to take a mindful moment that helps benefit your growing mind.

1. Find a comfortable place to sit or stand and set your timer for 8 minutes. Start the exercise with a round of 4 Square Breathing (page xii). Take a moment to look around your space. Notice the colors, sounds, smells, and objects in the space around you.

2. Do another round of 4 Square Breathing. Take a moment of acknowledgment: Consider what you learned today. Take a moment of appreciation: Consider what you feel successful about today. Take a moment of reflection: Consider what you accomplished today.

3. Do another round of 4 Square Breathing. Take a moment to shift your focus to the challenges of the day. Consider asking yourself, "What is the opportunity to learn from this challenge?" Or, "Is there another way I can look at this challenge?"

4. End the exercise with one final round of 4 Square Breathing.

GO DEEPER: As you head home today, take a moment to reflect on your day. Tonight, consider writing your responses to the exercise questions in your journal. Writing things down tends to reinforce and clarify your thoughts.

FOCUS

EXERCISE 38
Choice Chores

TIME TO READ: 2 MINUTES **TIME TO DO:** 8 MINUTES

Oh, no—now I have done it. I have brought up that unpleasant word: chores. Here is a little trick. When we choose to engage with our chores, they are not so much of a chore. We can turn an unpleasant experience into a pleasant experience when we actively choose to do so. Take a moment, choose a chore, and give this exercise a chance.

1. Pick your least favorite chore.

2. Set a timer for 8 minutes.

3. Remove any distractions (i.e., phone, TV, pets, etc.).

4. Start with 2 + 4 Breathing (page xiii). Repeat it four times, staying focused on your breath.

5. Focus on the chore you have chosen.

6. Take a moment to visualize completing the chore; visualize each step of completing the chore.

7. Do another round of 2 + 4 Breathing. Repeat four times, staying focused on your breath.

8. Now, actually begin working on the steps of your chore and pay attention to every detail.

9. Notice how your body moves. Stay in the moment, keeping the end result—completion of the chore—in the present.

10. Take a moment to think about the completed task and appreciate the outcome.

GO DEEPER: Sometimes music can help an unpleasant activity become more pleasant. Play your favorite artist. Have a dance party as you complete the chore. See if this helps increase the pleasant thoughts you experience about the chore.

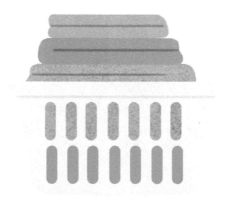

EXERCISE 39
Babbling Brook

TIME TO READ: 2 MINUTES   **TIME TO DO:** 8 MINUTES

When someone asks you how are you, do you ever really stop to consider the question? Like most people, you likely respond without really considering how you *do* feel. This mindfulness activity can help you learn to be connected to your feelings, bring them into awareness, and accept or tolerate them in new ways.

1. Walk around outside and find a small pebble. Pick up the pebble and roll it around in your hand. Set your timer for 8 minutes and start a round of 4, 7, 8 Breathing (Yoga Breath; page xi).

2. Imagine standing at the edge of a babbling brook. Notice the sunlight dance along the water. Notice dropping the pebble into the brook. Notice any thoughts, feelings, or sensations in your body.

3. Next, imagine seeing the pebble drop further down into the brook. Notice any change in your feelings, thoughts, or body sensations. Let the pebble settle at the bottom of the brook. Notice whether you can still see where it settled. Ask yourself, "What do I think, feel, or sense at this moment?"

4. Notice a small fish pick up the pebble with his mouth and swim upward. Do you notice any feelings rising into your awareness? Stay a little longer and watch the water babble down the brook.

5. End the exercise with a round of 4, 7, 8 Breathing (Yoga Breath).

GO DEEPER: Do you feel more connected to your feelings? Did you discover any feelings that you didn't realize were there today? Next time you do this exercise, listen to meditative music and notice the difference in your feelings after the exercise.

EXERCISE 40

Be, Not Bee

TIME TO READ: 2 MINUTES   **TIME TO DO:** 8 MINUTES

Sometimes to release the worried mind, we need to enter a state of simply *being*. We can then respond with acceptance of how things are and enter into a state of gratitude and joy. The worried mind, at times, can seem like a humming hive of bees. As we learn to be aware, we can learn to respond differently to worried thoughts and quiet them.

1. Find a comfortable place to BE. Sit comfortably, relax your body, and set your timer for 8 minutes. Start with a round of 2 + 4 Breathing (page xiii).

2. **B:** Breathe.

3. **E:** Expand your awareness of your body. Notice how your body is resting. Bring awareness to how your body feels in a seated position, noticing how your body feels with each breath in and out.

4. **B:** Breathe.

5. **E:** Ease into a more relaxed state. With every inhalation, relax more deeply into your body, pulling in the awareness of your space. With every breath hold, catch your thoughts. With every exhalation, release all the thoughts in your mind.

6. **B:** Breathe.

7. **E:** Enter into a moment of joy and gratitude. Notice how the sensations of joy and gratitude feel in your body.

8. **B:** Breathe.

9. **E:** Expand joy and gratitude to those around you. Extend your hands outward as if giving joy and gratitude to those around you.

10. End the exercise with a final round of 2 + 4 Breathing.

GO DEEPER: Take a moment of gratitude before you perform the exercise. Think of four things you are grateful for experiencing, knowing, or having. After the exercise, share your gratitude list with one of your friends. Notice how they respond. Do you respond differently to your list after you share it with someone else?

Part III
Mindfulness at Night

What Are Your Evenings Like?

You did it. You've conquered the day. You should feel light, accomplished, and ready for an epic snooze. Don't worry if you have any unfinished business lingering in your mind; mindfulness can help you gain peace.

As you may have guessed, many of the exercises in this book are a form of meditation. Studies find that people who meditate regularly have less cortisol in their bodies. Cortisol is that stress hormone I mentioned earlier. It's energizing and stimulating—great for running from danger, but it's not your friend when you have too much in your body at night and can't slow down. High cortisol has another downside: It is a memory squasher.

Mindfulness meditation in the evening can flush away cortisol to help you come back to the world the next day ready to absorb information like a sponge and achieve peak performance.

Isn't it amazing how our brains can change our whole state of being? I invite you to use mindfulness at night to restore your warm inner glow, deepen your sleep, and lift your overall mood.

COMMITMENT WILL HELP YOU SUCCEED!

Do your actions match up with your commitment to change? Knowing what is important can help you take actions to make lasting change—change that can bring you what you desire, making your life meaningful and pleasant. Committing to change will lead to the life you want.

Let's say that you value good grades. You can commit to creating time to focus on your studies by reducing or eliminating things that take time away from studying. Incorporating mindfulness into your life can help you commit to that change.

Remember: You aren't going to meditate for hours every day. You are going to meditate for 10 minutes a day. Before you know it, meditation will become a part of your daily routine.

EXERCISE 41
Gratitude Growth

TIME TO READ: 1 MINUTE   **TIME TO DO:** 9 MINUTES

Many people work on a daily affirmation or gratitude list first thing in the morning. Switching this to a nighttime ritual can be a soothing and calming task. Going to sleep with gratitude can help gratitude grow. You may find that you think about this gratitude list as you fall asleep.

1. Find a comfortable place to sit with a pen and paper to write. Set a timer for 9 minutes. Start the exercise with a round of 4 Square Breathing (page xii). As you breathe, allow your mind to become clear and calm. Reflect on your day.

2. Consider the pleasant and unpleasant moments. Write down your thoughts of gratitude in this way: "I am grateful for ___."

3. Notice your body for a moment. Write down your thoughts of gratitude for how your body served you today.

4. Consider the unpleasant moments and how they could have been worse. Write down your gratitude that the unpleasant moments were not that unpleasant and, actually, tolerable.

5. End the exercise with a round of 4 Square Breathing.

GO DEEPER: Did you notice a difference doing this exercise in the evening? Consider doing it 10 minutes before bed every night for one week. At the end of the week, write in your journal about how you felt doing this activity for a full week.

EXERCISE 42

Procrastination Pit

TIME TO READ: 2 MINUTES   **TIME TO DO:** 8 MINUTES

Do you ever find you avoid doing certain things? It is perfectly natural to procrastinate on doing certain things, especially when the action or activity doesn't bring you joy. This meditation helps you get out of that procrastination pit and focus on getting the task done.

1. Sit in a comfortable position and set a timer for 8 minutes. Start with a round of 2 + 4 Breathing (page xiii). On each exhale, relax and loosen a different part of your body—start with your shoulders and work your way down. Now, consider a task you have been putting off. Consider your reasons and excuses for putting off doing this task.

2. Do another round of 2 + 4 Breathing. Consider the negative impact that putting off this task could have on your life.

3. Do another round of 2 + 4 Breathing. Think about the benefit of getting the task done. Create an affirmation that could help you get to work on the task, such as "Starting it today means I am closer tomorrow to having it completed." Or, "I can do the things I have been putting off and I know I will feel much better when I do." Repeat your affirmation four times.

4. Do another round of 2 + 4 Breathing. Imagine all the steps of completing the task and see yourself doing the task. Imagine feeling light and at ease as you complete the task. Imagine the sense of accomplishment you'll feel when you've completed the task. Imagine how great it feels to have the task finished.

5. Finish the exercise with one final round of 2 + 4 Breathing.

GO DEEPER: Could you visualize completing the task? Were you able to find the reasons you have been putting off this task? Consider writing down the steps you visualized for completing the task. Commit to starting on the task in the next 24 hours.

EXERCISE 43
Silencing Stories

TIME TO READ: 3 MINUTES   **TIME TO DO:** 7 MINUTES

Do you ever find you are quick to point out the things that went wrong in your day? Do you keep coming back to the drama more than the joy? Sometimes, the best way to silence the negative stories in our life is to feel the feelings, let them pass, and reflect on the positive ones, or create positive intentions. This exercise helps you draw positive feelings forward.

1. Sit comfortably in the Half Lotus (crisscrossed legs) position. Hold your hands in half-Cs, with your fingertips touching in front of your body. Set your timer for 7 minutes and start a round of 4, 7, 8 Breathing (Yoga Breath; page xi).

2. Focus your awareness on your heart. Begin to scan your inner world for *negative* thoughts and feelings. Allow these feelings from the day to wash over you. Breathe into them, feel them, and let them become part of your whole being. Feel the sensations of the feelings.

3. Do another round of 4, 7, 8 Breathing (Yoga Breath).

4. Focus your awareness on your heart. Begin to scan your inner world for *positive* thoughts and feelings. If you are having difficulty accessing these feelings, consider how grateful you are for the space in which you are sitting, the

clothing you are wearing, and the food you have eaten today. Allow any positive feelings to emerge and wash over you. Breathe into them, feel them, and let them become part of your whole being. Feel the sensations of the feelings.

5. Do another round of 4, 7, 8 Breathing (Yoga Breath).

6. Notice where you feel the feelings. Do the feelings have a temperature or color? Do they move through your body? Imagine your body becoming warm and light. Gently smile.

7. End the exercise with a final round of 4, 7, 8 Breathing (Yoga Breath).

GO DEEPER: Were you able to notice a difference in how it felt to move from an unpleasant to a positive feeling state? Consider writing down the positive feelings on Post-it Notes and placing them around your room. Before going to sleep tonight, repeat, to yourself or out loud, the positive feelings you experienced and identify three things you are grateful for today.

EXERCISE 44
ABCs

TIME TO READ: 2 MINUTES   **TIME TO DO:** 8 MINUTES

It is human nature to avoid negative feelings. The problem with this is it can lead to sadness, decreased motivation, and anxiety. Here is another exercise to help promote kindness and compassion to accept your discomfort with distressing feelings.

1. Set your timer for 8 minutes. Lie on your bed and slowly begin to relax your body. Start a round of 4, 7, 8 Breathing (Yoga Breath; page xi).

2. **A:** Accept the day by focusing your attention on your head and your heart. Place one hand over your heart and one hand over your forehead. Notice any feelings you have about your day.

3. **B:** Breathe into the feelings.

4. **C:** Create compassion for the difficult feelings that emerge. Thank your heart and mind for handling the day. Take a moment of compassion by noting the more difficult or unpleasant feelings and say to yourself or out loud, "I feel (insert emotion) and I send you compassion and understanding."

5. Repeat until you have acknowledged and released all unpleasant feelings from the day.

6. End with a round of 4, 7, 8 Breathing (Yoga Breath).

GO DEEPER: Do you feel lighter? Consider purchasing a Tibetan singing bowl to play before and after this activity. Tibetan singing bowls create a range of sounds to help restore normal vibration frequency to the body and help bring the body into harmony. They are very soothing to the mind and soul.

EXERCISE 45

Clear and Calm

TIME TO READ: 3 MINUTES   **TIME TO DO:** 7 MINUTES

When you have had a long day filled with lots of physical or mental activities, it is helpful to prepare yourself for a good night's sleep by clearing and calming your mind. This is one of my favorite meditations. It brings such a deep sense of peace and relaxation. I almost feel a warm glow at the end of the exercise. Take a moment to enjoy the calm feelings.

1. Find a comfortable place to lie down and settle. Set your timer for 7 minutes. Close your eyes and allow your breath to relax you. Start the exercise with a round of 4 Square Breathing (page xii).

2. With your eyes open, inhale deeply through your nose. Hold, and notice your body. As you exhale, close your eyes. As you inhale, open your eyes. Hold, and notice your body. As you exhale, close your eyes and feel your whole body relax. Repeat four times.

3. As you inhale, feel your lungs fill with air. Hold, and notice your body. As you exhale, feel your lungs empty of air. As you inhale, imagine a wave of calm and peace washing over you. Hold, and notice holding the calm state. As you exhale, imagine any stress, worries, or anxiety leave your body as your lungs empty.

4. As you inhale, bring in confidence. Hold, and notice the confidence build. As you exhale, breathe out any doubts.

5. As you inhale, deepen the relaxation you feel and feel your body fill with positive feelings. Hold, and notice the positive feelings. As you exhale, let any heavy feelings or thoughts leave your body. Notice your mind becoming clear.

6. Repeat this affirmation four times: "I am calm. I am content. I am happy."

7. End the exercise with a round of 4 Square Breathing.

GO DEEPER: Do you feel calm and relaxed? Next time, listen to some meditative music while doing the exercise. YouTube has a number of free relaxing videos you can use.

EXERCISE 46
Teeth Time

TIME TO READ: 3 MINUTES   **TIME TO DO:** 7 MINUTES

Often we walk through life doing daily tasks without much thought. We become almost robotic in completing these tasks. A simple way to increase our concentration and focus is learning to be fully present with seemingly mundane daily tasks. Brushing your teeth is a great way to practice mindfulness.

1. Take a moment to ground yourself in front of your bathroom mirror and look at yourself in the mirror. Rub your tongue across your front teeth, noticing the sensation. If you notice your mind wander, it is okay to bring yourself back and notice your breath.

2. Set your timer for 7 minutes and start a round of 4, 7, 8 Breathing (Yoga Breath; page xi). Pick up your toothbrush and toothpaste, noticing the weight and the sensation of holding these objects. Apply the toothpaste to your toothbrush, noticing how it feels as the toothpaste comes out of the tube.

3. Do another round of 4, 7, 8 Breathing (Yoga Breath). Take a moment to smell the toothpaste. Begin brushing your teeth, noticing the sensation of the toothbrush passing over each tooth and the inside of your cheek and across your gums. Spit out the toothpaste and rinse your mouth. Notice the sensation before, during, and after you have spit and after rinsing your mouth.

4. Do another round of 4, 7, 8 Breathing (Yoga Breath). Rub your tongue across your front teeth, noticing the sensation after brushing. Now, brush your tongue and notice the sensations. Rinse your mouth once more and notice the sensations.

5. Finish with a final round of 4, 7, 8 Breathing (Yoga Breath).

GO DEEPER: Were you able to stay present or did your mind wander? What did you notice? Take a moment to consider your feelings and write them down in your journal. Next time, add flossing to the exercise and stay mindful and aware of it as well. Brush and floss your teeth for a full 10 minutes.

EXERCISE 47
Tiger Time

TIME TO READ: 2 MINUTES   **TIME TO DO:** 8 MINUTES

Did you know that those who have the tiger personality type are considered brave, confident, and liked by others? These are great character traits you can connect to by taking a Tiger Time moment. Engage with this exercise to see if you can allow these pleasant character traits to rise within you.

1. Set a timer for 8 minutes and stand in a comfortable position. Start the exercise with a round of 4 Square Breathing (page xii). First, stretch toward the sky as if a tiger is stretching up on a tree trunk. Next, kneel with your knees apart and stretch your arms as far forward as you can. Bend your elbows and move your weight forward onto your hands, almost with a thrust. Now, straighten your elbows and round your back while slightly pulling your belly button in and up toward your back. Kneel with your knees apart and stretch your arms as far forward as you can.

2. Do another round of 4 Square Breathing. Say to yourself or out loud, "May I be brave, confident, and well liked." Bend your elbows and move your weight forward onto your hands, almost with a thrust. Now, straighten your elbows and round your back while slightly pulling your belly button

in and up toward your back. Kneel with your knees apart and stretch your arms as far forward as you can. Say to yourself or out loud, "I am brave, confident, and well liked."

3. End with another round of 4 Square Breathing. Repeat the exercise until the timer completes.

GO DEEPER: Were you able to connect with some tiger personality traits? Do this exercise nightly for one week. At the end of the week, write in your journal about the difference in your connection with the traits of confidence and bravery.

EXERCISE 48

Relation Nation

TIME TO READ: 3 MINUTES   **TIME TO DO:** 7 MINUTES

Taking a moment to normalize our feelings can help us avoid being overwhelmed by the negative ones that can lead to anxiety or depression. Research has shown that people often remember negative feelings more than positive ones. By normalizing both positive feelings and negative feelings, we can lessen the impact of the latter.

1. Find a comfortable place to sit with both feet placed firmly on the ground. Set your timer for 7 minutes. Start with a round of 2 + 4 Breathing (page xiii). Imagine a light forming over your head, filling you with a sense of peace, joy, love, and compassion. Visualize the light moving into the center of your chest, bringing you a sense of health and healing.

2. Do another round of 2 + 4 Breathing. Draw out any negative feelings, discomfort, challenges, or worries you have. Picture all these difficulties as a dark cloud. With each inhale, imagine you are breathing this dark cloud into the white light until the dark cloud is completely absorbed into the white light.

3. Do another round of 2 + 4 Breathing. With each exhale, imagine that all the darkness is released. Feel joy, peace, and relief wash over you as the darkness is released. Imagine that your heart is flooded with light and that light begins to spill into every area of your body, filling you with love, contentment, and happiness.

4. Finish with a round of 2 + 4 Breathing.

GO DEEPER: Did you notice the sensations of your body as you drew out and acknowledged the unpleasant feelings? Next time, after you've completed the exercise, lie down and practice diaphragmatic breathing for 5 minutes. Once you complete the breathing, note whether you feel any other pleasant sensations or positive mood states.

EXERCISE 49
Zen Zone

TIME TO READ: 3 MINUTES   **TIME TO DO:** 7 MINUTES

Have you ever had a day when memories or anticipation of something enjoyable had your mind racing? Sometimes it is really hard to quiet our mind, especially when we are excited about something. This exercise will help you drift off to sleep and get a good night's rest. As you go through this exercise, you might notice some vibration, pressure, or other sensations. Be curious about them.

1. Lie comfortably in your bed. A timer is not necessary. Start the exercise with a round of 4 Square Breathing (page xii). Begin by noticing sensations at the top of your head. Allow your attention to notice your skull as it makes contact with the bed or the pillow. Notice the specific parts of your face. Next, notice your shoulders. If there is tension, release it and relax more fully into your bed. If anything feels extremely tense, breathe gently, directing the breathing into that area to allow it to soften.

2. Do another round of 4 Square Breathing. Let your attention move down your right arm. Notice any vibration, tingling, pressure, or movement as you reach your elbow, your lower arm, and then your hand. Notice your hands and fingers. Be curious about any sensations. Soften your hands and arms and release any sensations. Repeat with your left arm.

3. Begin to zigzag across your back, noticing any strong sensations or pressure points contacting the bed. Stay curious, release, and sink more deeply into the bed. Gently

scan your chest, down to the upper rib cage and into the stomach area. Breathe deeply, directing some breath into your stomach, allowing it to soften and relax.

4.   Do another round of 4 Square Breathing. Notice your pelvis and your hips. Bring attention to the places where your body connects with the bed, feeling whatever sensations are present. Start to bring the awareness down your right leg, noticing the sensations in your thigh, and circle your attention gently around the leg to your ankle, foot, and toes. Wiggle your toes, releasing the last bit of tension from the day. Repeat with the left leg and finish by breathing into your legs; hold kindness and curious attention to your legs for carrying you through your day.

5.   End with one final round of 4 Square Breathing.

GO DEEPER: Do you feel relaxed? Next time, consider scanning your body twice. Once you finish at your feet, restart the scan from your feet and go back up through your body until you reach the top of your head. Feel free to scan your body up and down as many times as is helpful to you.

EXERCISE 50
Mind Map

TIME TO READ: 3 MINUTES   **TIME TO DO:** 7 MINUTES

Mind maps can help you focus your attention on an idea or central topic by creating connections. The idea or topic is in the middle of the map with connections or other ideas extending off like branches from a tree. This technique has been proven to help you focus your attention and remember information through the use of words, images, numbers, and colors arranged in a fun way.

1. Find a comfortable place to sit and write. Set a timer for 7 minutes. Start the exercise with a round of 4 Square Breathing (page xii).

2. Write the idea or topic you want to develop further in the center of the paper. You can draw a box or a circle, or an image to represent the idea or topic. Draw branches coming out from the center. Begin by brainstorming. Think about your topic and allow ideas and thoughts to come to mind. Write them down on the branches.

3. Explore all the topics or subtopics or sub-ideas. If you have one, draw a branch off the main branches to write it in. Draw some images to reflect keywords or themes.

4. When the timer completes, focus on what you created with a closing round of 4 Square Breathing.

GO DEEPER: How did you like this exercise? Were you able to focus and come up with some good information? Consider listening to the TED Talk by Tony Buzan—the developer of Mind Maps—to learn more. Next time, use the full 10 minutes for this activity.

EXERCISE 51
Sky

TIME TO READ: 3 MINUTES   **TIME TO DO:** 7 MINUTES

Life isn't always roses and kittens. We cannot say at any one moment, "I've achieved everything and all my hopes and dreams are 100 percent fulfilled." However, if we take a moment, we can connect to some positive moments and experiences.

1. Lie on your bed and set a timer for 7 minutes. Start with a round of 2 + 4 Breathing (page xiii). Close your eyes. Feel your bed cradle every part of your body. Sink into the bed and feel every muscle from your toes to your head. Allow each muscle to relax and notice any sensations.

2. Imagine flying into the sky. Take a look down at Earth. Notice the trees and the colors of the sunset. Imagine you are floating around in the sky through the clouds. Imagine that, soon, you are flying over a place that feels peaceful, calm, and happy—this is your comfortable space.

3. Start another round of 2 + 4 Breathing. Use your senses to discover this comfortable space—its sounds, smells, and elements—such as a waterfall or a brook. Notice the colors you see in this comfortable space. Take a moment to land in this comfortable space. Find a place in your space to lie down and enjoy it. Notice the emotions and sensations you feel. Take a moment to say, to yourself or out loud, what you feel in this space.

4. End with a final round of 2 + 4 Breathing.

GO DEEPER: When you open your eyes, consider taking out your journal. Describe what your special place looks like, smells like, and feels like. What colors did you see? Were there plants? Trees? Animals? Next time you do this activity, use the full 10 minutes and see if you can find a new comfortable space to visit and describe.

EXERCISE 52
Worrywart

TIME TO READ: 2 MINUTES   **TIME TO DO:** 8 MINUTES

Sometimes one worrisome thought can cause another thought to pop up and increase our overall anxiety. People sometimes call a person who worries a *worrywart*. Actual skin warts are not fun and rather unpleasant. Sometimes you may feel like your worries are warts. One way to let go of your worries is to schedule a time to allow yourself to worry. Being mindful of containing your worries is an effective tool for moving through life without your worries being an unpleasant cloud that hangs around all day and pops up at inopportune times.

1. Pick a time of day, at least one hour before bedtime, to use as your worry time. Find a comfortable place to sit and set a timer for 8 minutes. Start with a round of 2 + 4 Breathing (page xiii).

2. Get out a clean piece of paper and write down your worries. You can worry as much as you want to worry— write it down. Even if they seem silly, write down those worries.

3. When the timer completes, rip up the paper and throw it away.

4. End with a round of 2 + 4 Breathing.

5. Now, go for a walk or engage in a pleasant activity.

GO DEEPER: How did you do? Did you notice a sense of relief as you tore up your worries? As you go through each day, if worries arise, tell yourself, "It is okay. I will address this in my worrywart time." Next time, instead of writing out your worries, talk them out with a trusted friend who will just let you vent for the full 10 minutes without interrupting. You can also talk about your worries out loud to yourself.

EXERCISE 53
Sleepy Sloth

TIME TO READ: 2 MINUTES   **TIME TO DO:** 8 MINUTES

A sloth is a curious creature that takes its time and seems at peace and happy. When you have made it through a tough day but find you are tense and can't wind down your mind, the Sleepy Sloth exercise is your ticket to a good night's sleep. Many of my teen clients have told me this is the one tool they use all the time. They have reported better sleep and a more relaxed state of being in the morning.

1. Turn off the lights in your room. You do not need a timer for this exercise. Walk ever so slowly to your bed; think of yourself as caught in a slow-motion movie scene. Slowly climb into bed.

2. Comfortably lie on your back. Place your hands over your belly button so you feel your diaphragm rise and fall as you breathe. Start the exercise with a round of 4 Square Breathing (page xii).

3. Now, tense all parts of your body—from your toes to your head. For example, curl your toes, flex your feet, lock your legs and arms, clench your fists, and lock your jaw. Slowly

release every muscle starting with your toes. Work slowly up your body, noticing each muscle relax. Repeat the exercise until you feel relaxed.

4. Once you are done, set a positive intention for the next day—for example, "Whatever the day holds, I will choose to be peaceful."

GO DEEPER: Mentally reflect on the experience before going to sleep. Consider and notice your mood. The next evening, take a moment to reflect on how setting a positive intention the night before affected your day.

EXERCISE 54
Arising Awareness

TIME TO READ: 2 MINUTES   **TIME TO DO:** 8 MINUTES

Increasing awareness of the world around you can help improve your focus. This exercise will help you keep your focus on the present moment. If you notice your mind start to wander, it is okay. Return to focusing on your breath and resume the awareness exercise.

1. Find a comfortable place to sit in Half Lotus (crisscrossed legs) position. Set a timer for 8 minutes and start a round of 4, 7, 8 Breathing (Yoga Breath; page xi). Bring your awareness to your mind and body. In this moment, become aware of the thoughts you have carried with you through this day to this moment. Take a moment to acknowledge these thoughts. Don't judge—just nod as you acknowledge them. Bring yourself back to your breathing. Breathe deeply, allowing your diaphragm to rise and fall. Focus on your breathing.

2. Start another round of 4, 7, 8 Breathing (Yoga Breath). Bring your awareness to your mind and body. In this moment, become aware of the feelings you have carried with you through this day to this moment. Take a moment to notice any sensations in your body. Nod as you acknowledge each sensation. Notice whether they change in the moment. Notice any tension or tightness in your

body. Breathe deeply in and out. Notice any noises in this space. Without judgment, just acknowledge and nod at each noise. Now, take a moment to notice any thoughts that rise and form. Notice how the mind allows thoughts to rise and then change to other thoughts.

3. End the session with a final round of 4, 7, 8 Breathing (Yoga Breath).

GO DEEPER: Were you able to bring yourself into the present moment? Take a moment to write in your journal about whatever came up with your thoughts and feelings and body sensations. Next time, increase the exercise time to the full 10 minutes.

RECONNECT

EXERCISE 55
Purposeful Pause

TIME TO READ: 2 MINUTES   **TIME TO DO:** 8 MINUTES

This exercise challenges you to engage in a purposeful pause in your digital world. There is emerging research that shows that all our time scrolling through and being on our phones can decrease the quality of our sleep and increase a sense of feeling overwhelmed.

Often we use our phones for connecting with friends, to take a break from an unpleasant activity, or to give us a sense of comfort from unpleasant feelings. Scrolling on your phone can cause you to disconnect from the present moment. Taking a purposeful pause every night is an opportunity to connect to the present; it might also give you a better night's sleep.

1. Lie on your bed and set a timer for 8 minutes. Turn on a pleasant instrumental music station or YouTube channel. Find a point on your ceiling to focus your attention. Start with a round of 2 + 4 Breathing (page xiii).

2. Focus on the rise and fall of the sounds in the music. Notice any body sensations or feelings that emerge as you listen to the music. Acknowledge them without judgment.

3. When the timer completes, end with a round of 2 + 4 Breathing.

GO DEEPER: How did you do? Did any unpleasant feelings come up? Next time, do the exercise for the full 10 minutes at least 30 minutes before bed. Leave your phone alone for the rest of the evening. The next morning, take a moment to reflect. Did you sleep a little better?

EXERCISE 56
Boxes

TIME TO READ: 3 MINUTES   **TIME TO DO:** 7 MINUTES

I bet there are times you pass through the day unaware of your thoughts and feelings. Increasing awareness can help you mindfully respond to them. When you walk through life disconnected, unpleasant thoughts and feelings can start to overwhelm you. This exercise will help you keep only the ones that give you joy.

1. Find a comfortable place to sit in Half Lotus (crisscrossed legs) position. Set a timer for 7 minutes and start a round of 4, 7, 8 Breathing (Yoga Breath; page xi). Bring your awareness to your mind. Notice any pleasant or unpleasant thoughts you had today. Nod and acknowledge the pleasant thoughts. Imagine placing the pleasant thoughts in a box with the label "gratitude" on it. Nod and acknowledge the unpleasant thoughts. Imagine the unpleasant thoughts as clouds that have dissipated as the wind gently carries them away. Notice a feeling of lightness as the unpleasant thoughts pass.

2. Do another round of 4, 7, 8 Breathing (Yoga Breath). Bring your awareness to your mind. Notice any pleasant or unpleasant feelings you had today. Nod and acknowledge the pleasant feelings. Imagine placing the pleasant feelings in the box labeled "gratitude." Nod and acknowledge the unpleasant feelings. Imagine the unpleasant feelings as clouds that have dissipated as the wind gently carries them away. Notice a feeling of lightness as the unpleasant feelings pass.

3. Do another round of 4, 7, 8 Breathing (Yoga Breath). Now, bring your awareness to your body. Notice any pleasant or unpleasant body sensations you have had today. Nod and acknowledge the pleasant sensations. Imagine placing the pleasant body sensations in the box labeled "gratitude." Nod and acknowledge the unpleasant body sensations. Imagine the unpleasant body sensations as clouds that have dissipated as the wind gently carries them away. Notice a feeling of lightness as the unpleasant body sensations pass. Take a moment to acknowledge and release the tension or tightness in each muscle, starting with your jaw and working down through your neck, shoulders, arms, and legs.

4. End with a final round of 4, 7, 8 Breathing (Yoga Breath).

GO DEEPER: Were you able to visualize placing the pleasant thoughts, feelings, and body sensations in the box? Were you able to allow the unpleasant ones to pass? Take a moment and draw a picture of your box with the various pleasant thoughts, feelings, and body sensations that have brought you gratitude.

EXERCISE 57

Peaceful Pastime

TIME TO READ: 3 MINUTES   **TIME TO DO:** 7 MINUTES

By now you might be starting to crave moments of calm meditation. Meditation can help you feel centered and at ease. Here is another peace-filled meditation to make you feel calm in the evening when your day is done.

1. Find a comfortable place to sit. Set a timer for 7 minutes and say out loud or to yourself, "The past is past. The future is future. I am concentrating on being happy, present, and peaceful." Concentrate on being aware of each breath and pay attention as your diaphragm rises and falls with each breath.

2. Start a round of 4 Square Breathing (page xii). Say out loud or to yourself, "I enjoy the here and now. I can stay in the here and now." Take a moment to embrace yourself and your breath almost like a mother embraces her baby.

3. Do another round of 4 Square Breathing. Say out loud or to yourself, "Thoughts rise and fall; that is their nature. I don't need to let them take hold of my mind. I am comfortable and at ease." Notice your body and your posture. Acknowledge your body, your posture, and any sensations you feel.

4. Stay connected to your breath as you inhale through your nostrils and exhale through your mouth. Do another round of 4 Square Breathing. Say out loud or to yourself, "I am aware of any tension and can release the tension." If there are sounds, do not react to them. Notice them and let them go. Say out loud or to yourself, "My body is free of tension. I am calm, rested, at peace. I feel free. I feel home."

5. Concentrate on being aware of each breath and pay attention as your diaphragm rises and falls. End the exercise with a final round of 4 Square Breathing.

GO DEEPER: Are you enjoying the benefits of meditation? Next time, pair this activity with a 5-minute stretching video from YouTube.

EXERCISE 58
Heartbeat

TIME TO READ: 2 MINUTES   **TIME TO DO:** 8 MINUTES

Take a moment to focus on your heartbeat. It can be a rep-
resentation of your feelings. Your heartbeat can help you
connect and focus on the present moment—especially in times
of stress or difficulty. You can also use your heartbeat, as well
as your breath, to draw you back to the present.

1. Set a timer for 8 minutes and lie on your bed. Feel your
    bed cradle your body. Take a moment to relax your
    muscles with your breath.

2. Start a round of 4, 7, 8 Breathing (Yoga Breath; page xi).
    Place your hand over your heart. Notice how quickly
    or slowly your heart is beating. Consider your current
    emotional state and how it might be connected to how
    your heart is beating.

3. Do another round of 4, 7, 8 Breathing (Yoga Breath).
    Begin to count backward from 100 by sevens. When you
    get to number two, take one large, deep inhale and feel
    your lungs fill with air. Begin to breathe normally. Draw

your attention back to your heartbeat, noticing if it is now slower or faster than before. Now, count as fast as you can to 100. Draw your attention back to your heartbeat, noticing if it is slower or faster this time.

4. Do a final round of 4, 7, 8 Breathing (Yoga Breath). Repeat until your timer completes.

GO DEEPER: Did your heartbeat change? Next time, do the exercise for a full 10 minutes and add noticing the rise and fall of your abdomen during the breathing section by resting a small pillow, stuffed animal, or other soft object on your abdomen. During the breathing cycles, pay attention to the rise and fall of your abdomen with the object.

EXERCISE 59

Changing the Past

TIME TO READ: 2 MINUTES   **TIME TO DO:** 8 MINUTES

Your past experience can influence how you feel today. For example, if you have ever gone to your room after a wonderful day and listened to music, there may be a song you associate with that day. The next time the song comes on, you might be instantly flooded with positive memories. This exercise is different but still audio related. It is designed to help you learn to listen nonjudgmentally and not be influenced as much by past experiences.

1. Find a comfortable place to sit. Set a timer for 8 minutes. Either put on earphones, or go into a room not affected by other sounds, and start a round of 4 Square Breathing (page xii).

2. Turn on a music channel and keep changing the playlist or channel randomly to a count of 10. If possible, change the channel with your eyes closed. Draw yourself to full awareness of the various tones and sounds within the song. Try to separate the tones and stay neutral about what you hear in the song. Notice whether there are times the intensity of the sounds increases or decreases. Notice any sensations you feel in your body. Do you feel a sense of wanting to move any part of your body to the music?

3. Do another round of 4 Square Breathing. Try to distinguish the different instruments within the music. If the song has vocals, try to determine the emotion of those who are singing. Notice how many different people are part of the vocals. Hone in on the range and tone of the vocals.

4. Repeat the steps for one more song.

5. End the exercise with a final round of 4 Square Breathing.

GO DEEPER: Were you able to stay neutral in your feelings? Next time, repeat this exercise with three songs. Then, at the end of the exercise, write down a description of what you notice in your body. Notice whether you tried to associate any unpleasant or pleasant feelings with the music.

EXERCISE 60

Changing Channels

TIME TO READ: 2 MINUTES   **TIME TO DO:** 8 MINUTES

Have you ever noticed you have the ability to channel your thoughts and feelings? Be aware of your channels. Some thoughts and feelings can be nourishing or depleting. I consider depleting thoughts like bad reality TV. When you find your mind is full of depleting thoughts, change the channel. Do this activity to help you bring awareness to thoughts that are nourishing or depleting and, if needed, change the channel.

1. Find a comfortable place to sit with a pen and paper to write. Set a timer for 8 minutes. Start with a round of 2 + 4 Breathing (page xiii).

2. Now, press the pause button on your day. Write down a list of all the activities you completed—from the time you woke up until now. Take a moment to allow your body and mind to respond as you read the list. Write an "N" next to anything that felt "nourishing" and a "D" next to anything that felt "depleting." Consider what depleting activity you could swap for a nourishing activity. Or, consider whether you could alter a depleting activity to make it more nourishing.

3. Now, consider your inner critic. Were there self-critical thoughts you had today? If yes, take a moment and say to yourself or out loud, "There was that critic. I am changing the channel to find an announcer who can be kind and gentle with me."

4. End the exercise with a round of 2 + 4 Breathing.

GO DEEPER: Consider writing a letter of encouragement to yourself. Read it when you feel your inner critic speaking and change the channel.

Conclusion: Walking the Mindful Path

Keep Building Your Practice

Congratulations! You've learned a habit that can support you for a lifetime. Through mindfulness you can tackle any challenge life throws your way.

You have learned 60 exercises that will bring you calm, focus, centeredness, and a more positive way to react to life. You've explored the best time of day for these exercises—morning, midday, or evening. And you've learned that you can change your mood at any time through mindfulness.

With this new habit, you can exercise greater control over how the world makes you feel.

Finding Your Path

Remember that mindfulness is not about changing your entire life. It's about living with greater awareness so you can enjoy more moments every day. I encourage you to share and teach others what you've learned.

Just 10 minutes a day of mindfulness practice will deliver rewards. Mindfulness lights up parts of your brain that aren't activated when you live your life on autopilot. It improves your well-being, helping you fully engage in the present, worry less, and connect more deeply with others. It will improve your physical health by relieving stress and supporting deep and restful sleep. It will improve your mental health by anchoring you to inner calm.

Mindfulness delivers so many benefits. This book's exercises will help you make it a lifelong practice.

How to Learn More About Mindfulness

Here are some of my favorite go-to apps, books, and online resources for exploring the world of mindfulness.

Apps

Headspace App

This app has some great meditations that are easy to use and fun. I like that you can vary the exercise time based on what you like. You can also try the app for free before paying for the expanded version.

Calm App

The Calm app delivers on its name. This is the app I recommend to my patients for expanding their knowledge of calming mindfulness exercises. This app has some of my favorite guided sleep meditations as well. This app also has a paid version with even more resources, but there are a good number of meditations on the free version.

Books

The Happiness Trap by Russ Harris
If you read any book, other than this one of course, this is my pick. Honestly, I think this should be required reading in high schools throughout the world. This book helps you understand mindfulness-based concepts to better handle unpleasant thoughts and feelings and create a meaningful life. It is a great way to engage further with the concepts we have discussed at length in this book.

Mindfulness for Teen Worry by Jeffrey Bernstein, PhD
This book is full of great tools and easy strategies to help
reduce worry and anxiety. The ideas Dr. Bernstein presents
are practical and fun.

Mindfulness Journals

There are also some great mindfulness notebooks available.
My personal favorite is *The Mindfulness Journal: Daily Practices,
Writing Prompts, and Reflections for Living in the Present Moment*
by S.J. Scott and Barrie Davenport.

Online Resources

YouTube Guided Meditations
YouTube is a fantastic online resource for free guided
meditations. Search for calming guided meditations, sleep
meditations, or body scan meditations.

www.MindfulnessExercises.com
This website has tons of free worksheets and journaling
sheets, along with useful meditations.

Miscellaneous

*Mindful Living Card Deck: 56 Practices to Feel Calm, Balanced,
Happy & Present* by Elisha Goldstein, PhD
This card deck is a great tool to increase your mindfulness
habit in a fun and easy way. There are 56 cards that offer
simple mindfulness activities that will work anytime you need
a new idea for an activity. Pull a new card each week and practice it for a full week.

Index

Acknowledgments

Thank you to Jerome Front, my professor at Pepperdine University, who first introduced me to the concept of mindfulness. A bigger thank you to Dr. Stephen Dansiger at the Institute for Creative Mindfulness for providing inspiration for bringing mindfulness into my daily practice.

About the Author

Jennie Marie Battistin, MA, LMFT, is a licensed marriage and family therapist in the state of California. She graduated cum laude with a master's degree in clinical psychology from Pepperdine University in Malibu, California. Jennie Marie began her career working with teens at Burbank High School.

She was a facilitator for *Angst*, a documentary on anxiety that helped create a dialogue among students, teachers, and parents about the challenges of coping with anxiety.

As a mother of five grown children, she has a passion for helping teens and parents develop tools and resources to navigate challenges and mental health concerns. Jennie Marie is the founding director of Hope Therapy Center Inc. Marriage and Family Counseling of Burbank and Santa Clarita. She has plans to expand the center's offices to Orange County, California, and the state of Washington.